A G

Ways to Pro *ent*

Incredible Babies

A GUIDE AND JOURNAL OF YOUR BABY'S FIRST YEAR

*Ways to Promote Your Baby's Social, Emotional
and Language Development*

CAROLYN WEBSTER-STRATTON, PH.D.

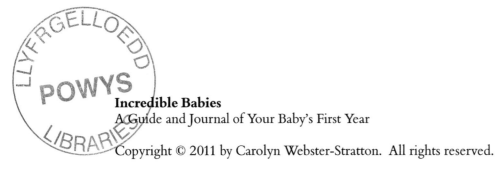

Incredible Babies
A Guide and Journal of Your Baby's First Year

Book design by Janice St. Marie

Webster-Stratton, Carolyn
Incredible Babies

Includes bibliographical references.
ISBN 978-1-892222-07-7

Publisher:
Incredible Years, Inc.
1411 8th Avenue West
Seattle, WA 98119 USA
206-285-7565
www.incredibleyears.com

Printed in USA

Acknowledgements

First, I am grateful to all those researchers who have been studying how babies think and learn. Perhaps the greatest giant was Piaget who first described the qualitative way babies' and children's thinking and cognitions change during critical developmental stages in their brain. In the past decade cognitive scientists have developed the technology to observe inside the baby's actual brain at their neuron connections and study the interplay of biology, genes and environment. While it is impossible to acknowledge all of this generation of scientists here, they cumulatively have helped us begin to understand how babies learn and what a difference a baby's supportive social environment can make to their physical, social and emotional development. They are helping us recognize and value the important job of nurturing parenting for the future of our children and the world.

Jamila Reid, my friend and colleague in my research and clinical work has read, commented upon and edited drafts of this book and I am very grateful for her wisdom and insights. Lisa St. George, director of Incredible Years business has helped make this book a reality by prodding me, proof-reading, copy editing, working with the graphic designer, and providing unfailing support.

And I end by acknowledging my family. My own parents taught me a great deal about commitment, caring, exploration and predictable routines, which in writing this book and thinking about my own childhood have taken on special importance in my mind. And as I have watched my own children now in their 20's develop, explore and persist with their goals to help families, I dedicate this to them and all others who work to care about and support families and their children. Finally, I thank my husband, who remains my anchor and supports my work with families.

CONTENTS

Chapter 4

Parents Learning to Read Babies' Minds   *111*

FIRST SIX MONTHS

Chapter 5

Parents Gaining Support   147

SIX TO TWELVE MONTHS

Chapter 6

Baby's Emerging Sense of Self   175

Foreword

I HAVE WORKED FOR THE PAST 30 YEARS as a pediatric nurse-practitioner and clinical psychologist. In this time a great deal of research has emerged regarding baby and children's brain development and how environment and genes interact in a synergistic way. While parents can't change the genes or particular temperament their baby arrives with at birth, it is clear that babies' brain wiring, circuitry, and eventual social, emotional, and academic competence is profoundly influenced by their environment, in particular by the way parents interact socially with them. Research and brain scans indicate that babies are incredible learners, primed by their brains to acquire information on their own and they have an enormous curiosity to learn. However, they come to us with "unfinished" and immature brains and while they have the full complement of neurons available at birth, the synapses or connections between the neurons are under massive construction and are flexible. In other words, babies are born with the raw brain structure material, but how it is put together in a healthy architectural form remains to be determined or sculpted by nurturing and responsive parenting interactions.

Babies' brain development seems to be a product of the "use it or lose it" principle; that is, neuron connections are strengthened by repetitive use and reinforcement and are weakened and may eventually disappear when they are not used. Parents and caregivers play a huge role in shaping their babies' brain development by their consistent and responsive parental responses to their babies' cues. One might think of the growth and development of healthy baby brains as similar to planting seeds in good soil and the gardener providing continual fertilization. As the plant grows, the weeds are removed and pruning is provided in order to get optimal growth. One must be cautious against too much pruning for fear of destroying the plant. The same might be said about parenting, the task is for parents to help their babies develop a strong brain foundation in soil which is rich with love, nurturing, coaching and healthy nutrients. This will strengthen the development of their social, physical, emotional, and cognitive brain neuron connections as well as babies' ability to form intimate, trusting relationships with others.

In this book I will discuss the first year of life and ways parents can become baby scientists by careful observation of their babies. Parents will learn to read their baby's internal states and subtle cues, and determine the optimal tactile, physical, visual, and responsive stimulation according to their baby's developmental stages, responses and needs. There is a rhythm and synchrony to this interaction, not unlike a tango dance. Responsive parents help their babies to acquire information from the outside world, to develop a sense of self, to develop strong parent-child attachments, and begin the on-going process of healthy emotional development. These crucial early life experiences with parents are laying down baby brain pathways that form the basis for later maturation of healthy social, emotional and language development.

I will discuss how babies develop from a more passive, observation learning modality to a more active exploration and interactive discovery learning of their environment and their sense of self. I will talk about ways parents can assure their babies' physical and emotional safety, provide adequate nutrition and healthy sleep patterns. Each chapter has a journal section where parents can keep record of things their babies have learned to do each month as well as capture their memories of their babies' likes and dislikes and their favorite activities, songs, stories and daily routines. I hope that this journal will be something you can share with other family members and care givers to let them know about your baby's needs and personality. Perhaps when your baby is older this will be something you can read together as children love to hear stories about themselves as babies. The time of babyhood passes much more quickly than you can imagine. When you are in the midst of responding to your baby's need to be fed or diaper changed every 2-3 hours, it may seem like you will never sleep again or have a moment to yourself, but soon your baby will be a talking, walking toddler. Capturing some of these early special times in this journal can help preserve your memory of your first year with your incredible baby.

Carolyn

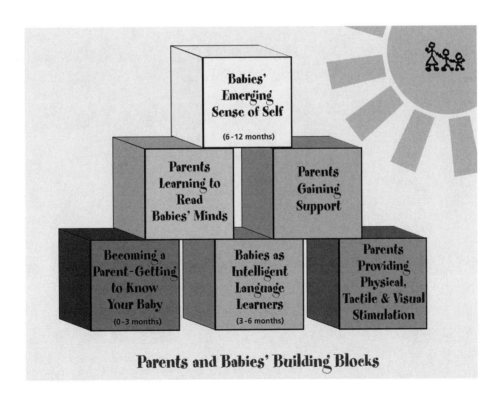

Parents and Babies' Building Blocks

CHAPTER 1

Becoming a Parent and Getting to Know Your Baby—

THE FIRST THREE MONTHS

Introduction

Babies are intelligent learners. Right from the first hours infants are observing, thinking, and even reasoning. They are highly attuned to their environment and are actively working to find out about the world they live in. Within a few days of birth, babies are able to discriminate human faces and voices from other sights and sounds. Did you know babies actually prefer the human face and human stimulation to anything else? Before they can even walk or talk, they can actually tell the difference between a face that is happy, sad, or mad. In fact, babies' brains seem to be programmed to recognize people who love them and to seek out human stimulation above all else.

In this book we will discuss the baby's first year of life and ways parents can become baby scientists through careful observation of their babies, learning to read their internal states and subtle cues, and determining the optimal tactile, physical, visual and communication according to their needs and responses. There is a rhythm and synchrony to this baby-directed interaction, not unlike a tango dance. In so doing parents are nurturing, responsive, and helping their babies in their incredible journey to develop a strong foundation or brain architecture for their future growth.

None of us are born knowing how to parent. And if you are a new parent, you may be overwhelmed by the many things there are to learn such as how to feed your baby, change her diaper, or bathe her. This book will help you learn some of those practical things, but it is also important to remember that you already have an incredibly valuable parenting tool—that is, the love you have for your baby. By observing your baby carefully, you will learn about your baby's unique temperament and how you can facilitate your baby's own intellectual, physical, social and emotional development. Most of all you will learn to trust your own wisdom about what your baby is telling you. In other words, let your baby teach you what she needs.

Learning to Communicate and Listen to your Baby

One of the most important learning tasks for both new and seasoned parents is to try to understand what your baby is communicating: you do this by trying to read the signals that your baby is giving you. One of the first ways a baby signals or communicates is by crying. You will learn to listen to your baby's cries and sort out a cry of distress, a cry for a diaper change, a cry of hunger, a cry of anger, or a cry signaling a need for some change in activity, stimulation, or scenery. Don't worry if you can't distinguish these different cries at first! It takes time to decode the meaning of these cries. Relax and give yourself time to watch, study, and learn this new baby language. Take time to listen to the different types of cries your baby has.

Observing and listening to baby

Sometimes parents feel confused about whether they are spoiling their baby if they respond to every cry. *Remember you cannot spoil your baby in the first 4 months of life.* In fact, it is important that babies have their cries responded to predictably during the first months. This can be a rather overwhelming task for parents since some babies are very fussy and cry a lot of the time. Parents will be meeting their baby's basic needs in a loving and responsive way by providing food, a dry diaper, a quiet place to sleep, and lots and lots of cuddling, holding, comfort, and communication. When these needs are consistently provided in the first year of life, a baby learns about trust and becomes securely bonded with her parent. That is, if your baby cries and you predictably come to help, your baby will feel secure. On the other hand, a neglected baby who cries and receives no response, or an unpredictable response from a parent, will develop a sense of mistrust or feel insecure about relationships.

Remember you cannot spoil your baby in the first 4 months of life.

A baby's crying may indicate a basic need for food, to be burped, or for a diaper change, but crying may also signal critical needs for physical, auditory, visual, and tactile stimulation. In fact, this kind of stimulation is as important for your baby as food.

Your baby's brain neuron connections are immature, and how you respond to her social and emotional cues will become part of the eventual architecture of her brain wiring and circuitry. Your relationship with her will shape the way her brain grows and the kind of person she will become.

In the first three months babies are primarily "observational learners"—they learn by observing you intently and listening and locking onto your face with their attention and eyes. You can be an observational learner during this time too. See what your baby likes to look at, listen to, and how she responds to different types of touch.

Eye contact – 12 inches

Newborn babies can only focus on objects within 8–15 inches of their nose. Therefore, when you are talking to your baby, place your face about 12 inches from her face, as this is optimal for your baby's visualization. It is important to talk to your baby as if she understands what you are saying. Smile and give your baby positive and caring feedback because your baby is capable of reading the emotions behind your words from your facial expression and tone of voice. This is important for your baby's language and social learning. By four months or sometimes even earlier, you can expect your baby to begin to take turns in conversations with you by cooing when you stop talking. You may also notice less crying and more coos and gurgles. Positive social and physical interactions with you during this time will be important not only in strengthening your attachment, but research indicates, also has the added benefits of increased baby growth and reduced stress physiological responses.

In addition to talking and listening to your baby, you can provide visual stimulation with toys, pictures, and household objects. When your baby is still too young to grasp the toys, you can hang or hold them about 12 inches from her face. Try not to offer too many toys at once because having too much in a baby's visual field may confuse or frustrate her. Giving your baby one

or two toys and then replacing them when she seems bored can help your baby focus and avoid her getting over stimulated. Pay attention to how much stimulation your baby can handle. There are wide individual differences in the way babies handle stimuli just as there are differences in babies' need for sleep, amount of crying and in how they can be soothed. The goal for parents is not to compare but to watch for, listen and respond sensitively to your own baby's unique style and in so doing, strengthen your baby's individual cognitive, language, social and emotional neural connections.

BABY ALERT
You cannot spoil your baby in the first 4-5 months by picking her up when she cries. In fact, this increases your baby's sense of security in her environment.

Managing Fussy Periods

Between three and twelve weeks most babies will have a fussy or crying period, usually toward the end of the day. Parents often find there is very little they can do to soothe or calm their baby during this time. This can be frustrating for parents, especially as it coincides frequently with the time when mothers and fathers are exhausted or returning home from work. In its extreme form this inconsolable fussy state is called "colic" and may last for three or more hours a day. About 15-20% of infants experience colic. But most other babies have shorter, distressed, crying periods every day. Because this fussing behavior is so clocklike in its predictability for most babies, it is thought to have an organizational purpose for the baby's immature nervous system. In fact, some (or many) fussy periods are to be expected, are a healthy sign, and contribute positively to baby's neurological development. Remember that your goal is to teach your baby that you are there for her, however, this doesn't mean that you need to hold your baby 24 hours a day or respond to every little peep. There will be times when you can't respond to your baby's cry immediately, don't worry that this will traumatize your baby for life. You will also need to develop some coping strategies for yourself and your baby in order to get through the fussy periods!

The best approach is to test out all the reasons you think your baby might be crying (wet diaper, hunger, sick, tired, too hot or cold, needs to burp, lonely or bored). If all of your baby's basic needs seem to be met, then try different comfort strategies such as holding, rocking, soft singing, dim lighting, walking, bouncing, swaddling, and wearing in a sling. Remember, when soothing or cuddling a fussy baby, it is important to remain calm, for babies can read your emotions and your anxiety will be felt by your baby. Remember, too, there will be times when holding and cuddling a fussy baby doesn't work to calm her down. Typical fussy periods will last no more than

Learning baby's crying signals

Typical fussy periods will last no more than 1–2 hours.

1–2 hours. If you become too anxious or barrage an already overloaded nervous system with more stimulation, it will be harder for your baby to calm down. If you have reassured yourself that your baby is not wet, in pain, ill, too hot or cold, or hungry, and if your comforting techniques are not working, sometimes it can be helpful to give your baby a break from all stimulation as well as a break for yourself.

During these fussy periods it is crucial that you have some support as a parent.

You can do this by swaddling your baby in a blanket and placing her in her crib in a dimly lit room. During this time, try to be patient, remain calm, and let your baby cry for 5–10 minutes to let off steam. You should stay nearby—either in the same room or right next door in order to monitor her ability to self-soothe. This is not letting your baby "cry it out." Rather, you are testing out the possibility that your child is so over stimulated by all the sights, sounds, and touch in her new world that she needs a break. After 5–10 minutes, you can go back and stroke your baby's head, or help her put her hands in her mouth to suck, and talk to her calmly or sing softly. Don't pick her up immediately. Notice if she is responsive to your soothing touch and voice. If not, you may hold her briefly and then put her down for another cycle of fussing. This routine is rarely needed more than 3–4 times. It is thought that after this fussing period is over, the baby is better organized and will sleep better. During these fussy periods it is crucial that you have some support as a parent. If you have a partner in parenting, take turns attending to your baby, so that the other parent can have a break. If you don't have a partner in parenting, find some ways to help yourself stay calm such as take a tea break or call a friend or do some relaxing breathing. Remember that although this fussiness is very hard to listen to, it is a normal developmental stage and most babies grow out of the worst of this by 4-5 months.

Stay calm, patient and relaxed

Thumb Sucking and Pacifiers

Avoid using a pacifier every time your baby cries.

Thumb sucking and pacifiers are healthy self-comforting methods for babies that help them manage times when they are fussy and irritable. Babies seem to have a built-in sucking reflex, which starts in utero. However, it is good to restrict the use of a pacifier to times when you have tried other soothing strategies and your baby still needs self-comforting. Avoid using a pacifier every time your baby cries. It is usually better to hold and rock your baby and to let her suck on her hands at first. By doing this you are helping your baby not become too dependent on the pacifier as the sole means for self-soothing.

Deciding Whether Your Baby is Sick

Temperature: Most doctors agree that a normal body temperature for a healthy baby is between 97 and 100.4 degrees Fahrenheit (36–38°C). Temperatures above that are considered a fever. Parents are the best judges of whether their baby is ill and should call their doctor if they are worried, even if there is no fever. Also, fever is more serious in babies under three months. If the baby is less than three months old and has a temperature of 100.4°F (38°C) or higher, call your doctor immediately. For a baby between three and six months, call if the temperature reaches 101°F (38.3°C) or higher. Over six months, call if fever reaches 103°F (39.4°C) or higher. One of the important things to consider is how your baby looks and behaves. Pay attention to how irritable she is, whether she is drinking and urinating, or whether she has skin color changes. You do not need to overdress or blanket a baby with a fever. This may actually heat up your baby. Instead take off some layers and let her rest in a cool spot.

BABY ALERT
Don't give your baby any over-the-counter medicine until you have talked with your doctor.

Baby Acne

Simply wash your baby's face with mild baby soap and water once a day.

Baby acne is very common and usually shows up sometimes in the first month on the cheeks and sometimes on the forehead or back. These small whiteheads might be surrounded by reddish skin and become more evident when the baby is hot or fussy. The acne may be caused by hormones that are released by the mother during the last week of pregnancy. This usually clears up on its own in a couple of weeks, but can sometimes linger longer. Do not put creams or oils on your baby's skin because this will  make the acne worse. Also avoid scrubbing or washing your baby's skin too much because baby acne is not caused by dirt. Simply wash your baby's face with mild baby soap and water once a day.

Soft Spot

Babies have one soft spot (fontanel) on the top of the head and a smaller one at the back. Sometimes the pulse beneath these spots can be seen. These areas are where the bones of the baby's skull have not yet grown together. This soft spot allows the skull to mold for delivery. This flexible skull also allows the brain to continue to grow during the early years of life. The rear spot closes within four months while the front one closes by one year. These spots can be touched gently and are covered by a tough membrane to protect the brain beneath. If the head gets a bang, the skull will give. It is an important protection but is less fragile than you might think.

Feeding

Even though breast milk is the perfect and recommended milk for babies, there are good reasons why some parents need to bottle feed rather than breast feed. Regardless of whether you bottle feed or breast feed, you can provide your baby with the close contact, nurturing, and intimacy that your baby needs during feeding times. During these feeding times the most important thing is to have face-to-face contact, look your baby in the eyes, cuddle her closely, talk to her while feeding, smile, and if you bottle feed, tilt the bottle upright so the nipple is full of formula.

You might have noticed there are two kinds of sucking: sucking which your baby uses to keep herself comforted and under control, versus nutritive sucking for hunger and feeding. The first type uses the front of the tongue in a licking motion and the second type uses the back of tongue and pulls from the back of throat. The baby will start sucking with short bursts of constant sucking–then a burst-pause pattern, then suck-suck pause. Often, pauses are a good time to play and talk–or, a good time to burp.

In the first months you will be preoccupied with feeding your baby. You might be concerned about whether your baby is getting enough milk, how long to feed or nurse at one time, and how to burp. If your baby is breast-fed, 15–20 minutes per breast will usually be enough for sucking and adequate milk. If your baby is formula fed, 1–3 ounces per feeding for a newborn is plenty. (The average baby takes 2–3 ounces per day for every 1 pound of body weight.) You can also tell if your baby is getting enough milk if your baby seems satisfied after feeding, is going 1–2 hours between feedings, urinating

often (wet diaper means your baby is hydrated), and after the first week, is gaining weight. Breast milk is the perfect food in the first 6 months and whether your baby is breast fed or formula fed, solid foods are not recommended until 6 months.

BABY ALERT
Don't try to follow rigid feeding schedules in the first weeks or months. Feeding can occur every couple of hours or "on demand" as often as your baby seems hungry.

Remember your baby's stomach is small and can't hold too much milk at one time. Don't worry about weight loss in the first week. Breast-fed babies can lose as much as 7 – 10% of their body weight in the first 4 – 5 days; a 5% weight loss is considered normal for formula-fed babies. After the first month, babies usually gain about half a pound a week.

BABY ALERT
If you are bottle feeding, never prop the bottle up and leave your baby to drink it unattended. This could cause choking. Your baby needs you to hold the bottle while she drinks.

Burping and Spitting

About 40% of young babies spit up regularly and the peak age is 4 months. Often after a noisy, gulping feeding, parents can expect a gush of milk to follow. It occurs because the baby gulps in air along with her breast milk or formula and the air gets trapped in the stomach. The air has to be released and brings some milk with it. While every baby is different, generally babies need to be burped midway through a feed and at the end of a feed. If your baby gulps a lot, then you may need to burp her more often. If you stop your feeding to burp midway and your baby cries, resume feeding. If your baby falls asleep nursing or taking a bottle, it's likely you don't need to wake her up to burp her. However, if she wakes up fussy a few minutes later, that's a good signal that she needs to burp. Otherwise, let her sleep and skip the burping.

Most babies stop spitting up around 6–7 months.

There is no one right way to burp babies, but generally burping involves taking the pressure off the stomach and holding the baby upright so the air will move up and out. You can do this by holding your baby over your shoulder with her chest against your chest patting her back. Or, you can sit your baby on your lap, support your baby's jaw while rubbing the baby's back. Or, laying your baby over your lap with her head on one side of your thigh will also work. If you have another position that works, keep using it.

Parents often worry about the quantity of milk that is spit up with a burp. However, it usually looks like much more milk is spit up than actually is. Try spilling a tablespoon of milk on the counter to see what it looks like. If your baby is not fazed by the spitting up and is gaining weight normally, then spitting up is nothing to worry about. Most babies stop spitting up around 6–7 months when they begin to sit up on their own or are crawling or walking.

Some Tips to Keeping Milk Down

- Hold your baby upright
- If bottle-feeding, make sure the nipple hole isn't too small or too big. A small hole will frustrate the baby and make her swallow air. A large hole will result in the baby gulping milk too quickly
- Stay calm and minimize distractions during feeding
- Take the opportunity to burp when your baby has a natural pause in feeding
- Don't worry if your baby doesn't burp every time you pat her, she probably doesn't need to
- Keep your baby calm and up right for 20 minutes after she eats and avoid too much activity

---

BABY ALERT

If your baby is distressed and spitting up large quantities of milk in a forceful or projectile manner, then this is vomiting and you should call your doctor or nurse. Also call your doctor right away if there is any bile in the vomit.

Too much spitting, frequent bowel movements between feedings, and dry eczema-type rash on the baby's face may be an indication of sensitivity to milk protein. Check with your doctor if this is occurring to see if your baby has a milk allergy and should be on soybean formula. Breast-fed babies usually do not have these milk intolerances.

Bowel Movements and Diaper Changing

A breast-fed newborn baby may have as many as 8–10 bowel movements (BMs) a day in the first week. In these first days, the bowel movements are thick and dark green to black in color due to the meconium that has built up during pregnancy. As the baby starts to nurse the bowel movements will turn yellowish. For breast-fed babies stools are yellow and seedish. After the first week, the BMs occur less frequently and by 4-6 weeks it is quite normal for a breast-fed baby to go a week without a bowel movement. Breast-fed babies do not become constipated.

A formula-fed baby starts with the black or dark green stools and then they change to yellow, tan, or greenish brown color. The newborn baby usually has one or more BMs a day and at 1–2 months of age can go up to several days between BMs. It is not how often a baby has BMs, but how hard the stool is that is the cause for concern. Normally the stool is a little firmer than a breast-fed baby's stool, about the consistency of peanut butter. Constipation is when the BM is hard, large, and difficult for the baby to pass. If a formula-fed baby has hard stools, or more than 5–6 green, mucousy, or watery stools, parents should check with their doctor.

A baby's BMs can vary color from day to day depending on what the breast feeding mother is eating, how hydrated the baby is, and type and frequency of formula if the baby is bottle-fed. When parents introduce cereal and other solids, there can be dramatic changes in color, odor and frequency of BMs. See chapter 6 for information about handling constipation during this transition.

BABY ALERT
Babies' bowel movements are as individual as babies are and over time parents will get to know their normal patterns.

Baby's Sleeping Patterns

Newborns sleep 17–18 hours a day in the first few weeks, and during the first 3-4 months babies spend more time asleep than awake. But this sleep usually occurs in shorter spurts and babies need to eat and have diaper changes frequently. It is not practical to try to have a rigid schedule in the first 3–4 months of your baby's life, and you will likely need to be flexible around your baby's naps.

However, by 4–5 months, most babies will be sleeping in longer intervals and have a more predictable sleep-wake pattern. At this age you can start setting up a more regular sleep schedule. But remember every baby is on a unique developmental schedule and your observations and records of your own baby's sleep patterns will give you cues to your baby's readiness for this.

Sleeping Through the Night: At some point between 4–6 months, most babies are capable of sleeping in stretches of 5–6 hours at a time. This may not sound like much if you were hoping for an 8–9 hour stretch, but it is an important milestone as it will allow you to begin to get several hours of uninterrupted sleep. By 6 months, if not before, your baby is ready for the night weaning, if you should choose to do that. See chapter 6 for information about setting up a bedtime sleeping schedule.

BABY ALERT

There should be no stuffed animals, pillows, lose blankets, pillow-like bumpers or small toys in cribs. Until babies learn to roll over they should always be placed in their cribs on their backs for naps or night time sleeping. Use a firm sleep surface, such as a safety-approved crib mattress, covered by a fitted sheet. Never place your baby to sleep on pillows, sheepskins or other soft surfaces.

Parents' Need for Sleep and Support

It is also important to adjust your expectations for yourself.

In the first few months, babies wake up several times a night to be fed. This means that you cannot get a full cycle of sleep and will frequently be tired. Indeed the unpredictability of your baby's sleep schedules and feeding needs will keep you on your toes. It will be important to be flexible, take advantage of your baby's naps to get some extra sleep yourself, go to bed early, or find the support of others who can watch your baby while you rest.  Getting support from your partner or friend or a family member can make all the difference. It is also important to adjust your expectations for yourself. Keeping a tidy house or cooking involved meals will be far less important than staying rested and being available to your baby for feeding, cuddling and playing. It is not possible to "do it all." Think about your priorities and the importance of putting your children first.

 BABY ALERT
Don't allow smoking around your baby.

Nurturing Babies' Brains with
Responsive Communication and Stimulating Activities

Babies come to us with "unfinished" and immature brains and while they have the full complement of neurons in place at birth, the synapses or connections between the neurons (electrical circuits) have not been determined, are flexible and are under massive construction. In fact, baby's brain connections are sculpted in some healthy and unique architectural form by parents having responsive and nurturing interactions with them. We have talked about how parents learn to decode their babies' crying signals and to understand whether they are asking to have their hunger satisfied, or their messy diapers changed, or whether their crying is signaling their need for some physical, auditory, visual, or tactile stimulation. This kind of stimulation is as important for your baby's eventual brain wiring and circuitry and physical development as feeding her. In fact, your communication and loving play interactions will shape the way your baby's brain grows and the kind of person she will become.

Body to body tactile touch

BABY ALERT
Always place bouncy seats on the floor. Never put the bouncy chair on the table or kitchen counter; even your baby's little movements could bounce it onto the floor.

Parents as Baby Scientists—To Sum Up . . .

So in the first months of your baby's life, you are a kind of a baby scientist; problem solving and sorting out the meaning of your baby's cries and cues. You check out your hypotheses regarding the various reasons your baby might be crying by changing her diaper, trying to soothe her with rocking or cuddling or using a pacifier, feeding her to see if she is hungry, or by checking her temperature or skin warmth and consulting your doctor. By responding in these predictable and sensitive ways you are helping your baby develop a sense of trust; that is, your baby is learning that when she is distressed she can trust you to try to help her. This helps her feel emotionally secure in her environment. Remember, right now, crying is the only way your baby has to communicate that she needs something, so your responses to her crying are important. It is normal for parents to have worries about their baby and to wonder if their baby's responses are normal. Sharing these worries with a partner, close friends, parent support group, or health care provider is a helpful way to get reassurance about what to do.

By the end of the first 3 months you will have learned a lot about your baby. You will have learned to read your baby's cues, emotions and behaviors. You will have begun to decode the language of your baby's cries. You will be able to interpret whether your baby's crying is an expression of a need for a diaper change, a hunger need, or a request for some attention. By playing, affectionately touching and telling your baby about your feelings for her, you are helping her feel loved. You have begun your life-long bond with your baby, and she has begun responding to you with gurgles, coos, and smiles. You will have begun to figure out whether your baby likes the bouncy chair better than the swing and which toys and songs make her smile.

Observing and listening to baby

You are thinking about your baby's point of view, adjusting the amount of stimulation your baby needs according to her individual responses and enjoying her.

It is important to be patient with yourself and give yourself time to learn this new baby language. As you first try to speak and understand your baby's language, you and your baby may both be frustrated. This is a reciprocal learning process for you and for your baby as each of you begins to interpret the other's form of communication. Remember just as you are a scientist, so is your baby a scientist. Babies are trying to figure out from your interactions what you are feeling, how their own actions affect you, and how to tell you what they want. Although it has only been a few months since your baby was born, you and your baby will have already learned a lot about each other and each of you have begun the bonding process.

It is important to be patient with yourself and give yourself time to learn this new baby language.

Points to Remember about
GETTING TO KNOW YOUR BABY

Every baby is different. Spend some time observing your baby and getting to know her temperament and how she reacts to your communication.

My baby and I learn from each other

- Look and smile at your baby—your face should be about 12 inches from your baby's face.
- Observe your baby's responses to your smiles and interactions.
- Listen to your baby's cries to sort out different kinds of cries: hunger cries, messy diaper cries, tired cries, illness cries, boredom cries, or over stimulation or need for stimulation cries.
- Watch how your baby responds to your cuddles , rocking, and affectionate touch.
- Watch how your baby responds to music.
- Sing to your baby.
- Talk to see if your baby turns her head in response to your voice.
- Talk to your baby when there is a pause in her feeding.
- Observe how your baby responds to black and white objects, color, objects with noises, and lights.
- Wear your baby on your chest in a sling and see how she responds.
- Respond to your baby's cues by trying out various ideas about what she may be trying to tell you.
- Look for self-soothing efforts your baby makes such as sucking her hands.
- Ask your partner what s/he is noticing about your baby.
- Keep a baby journal and jot down things your baby is interested in or developmental landmarks.

Points to Remember about
TAKING CARE OF YOURSELF

I'm keeping life simple

- Get as much rest as possible.
- Take naps—try to sleep when your baby sleeps.
- Give yourself a break—ask someone to watch your baby so you can nap.
- Do something nice for yourself such take a long bubble bath or walk with a friend.
- Share your joys and difficulties with another parent.
- Tell yourself you are doing a good job learning from your baby.
- Keep a log of the fun moments.
- Don't worry about a messy house or making fancy meals.
- Accept a meal from a friend.
- Use take-out for a special treat.
- Keep life simple.
- If you are breast feeding, you could pump a bottle of milk every day so a friend, partner, or other family member can take over a feeding.

Write your own favorite self-care activities here:

Parents' Viewpoint
HOW I WILL COPE WITH CRYING

If you know your baby's hunger and diaper needs have been met and you've tried to soothe and cuddle your baby but she is still crying and inconsolable, it's time to take care of yourself so you don't get too frustrated. Take 5–10 minutes to calm yourself.

  • Put my baby in a safe place and let her cry for 5–10 minutes

Stay nearby, but calm myself:
  • Put on quiet music to distract myself
  • Take deep breaths
  • Remind myself nothing is wrong with my baby—crying is normal and is her release as well as how she organizes herself
  • Tell myself, "It will get better in a few months"
  • Tell myself, "I can cope with this"
  • Don't take my frustration out on my baby by shaking her
  • Call someone for help if I feel my frustration building
  • Remember the crying or fussy period will usually end in 1-2 hours

After 5–10 minutes of relaxing, go back to my baby and rock and soothe my baby for a while, then put her down and repeat the above. Usually parents won't have to do this more than 3 or 4 times before the baby has calmed down.

I help my baby feel secure and safe

MY BABY'S JOURNAL

Write down notes here each week about your discoveries of your baby and the joys of babyhood.

My Baby's Journal
FIRST WEEK

SLEEP TIMES

FEEDING TIMES

PLAY & ALERT TIMES

FUSSY TIMES

BOWEL MOVEMENTS

My Baby's Journal
ONE MONTH

SLEEP TIMES

FEEDING TIMES

PLAY & ALERT TIMES

FUSSY TIMES

BOWEL MOVEMENTS

My Baby's Journal
TWO MONTHS

SLEEP TIMES

FEEDING TIMES

PLAY & ALERT TIMES

FUSSY TIMES

BOWEL MOVEMENTS

My Journal
THREE MONTHS

SLEEP TIMES

FEEDING TIMES

PLAY & ALERT TIMES

FUSSY TIMES

BOWEL MOVEMENTS

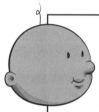

Baby's Viewpoint
THINGS I CAN DO (0–3 months)

Activity	Date	Observations/Comments
I follow objects with my eyes		
I do gurgles, oohs and ahs		
I smile and laugh and squeal		
I found my hands today		
I look at my parent's face		
I have a favorite toy or activity		

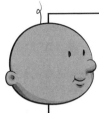

Baby's Viewpoint
THINGS I CAN DO (0–3 months)

Activity	Date	Observations/Comments
I can recognize my parent's voice		
I can hold my head up		
I sit in a wobbly way but need support		
I know my name		
I can say baba		
I like being read to		

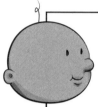

Baby's Viewpoint
THINGS I CAN DO (0–3 months)

Activity	Date	Observations/Comments
I found my feet		
I react when you are happy		
I love to be sung to		
I am imitating sounds		
I know when it is not you taking care of me		
I love to explore with my mouth		

First Three Months
BABY'S HAND AND FOOT PRINTS

Stamp your baby's hand
or foot here during the first three months.

First Three Months
BABY'S FIRST PICTURES

CHAPTER 2

Parents as Responsive Communicators and Babies as Intelligent Language Learners–

THE FIRST THREE MONTHS

Introduction

When do newborns start learning language? Actually babies know important things about language from the time they are born–and they learn a great deal about language before they can actually say anything. As we have discussed in Chapter 1, in the first month your baby is keenly attuned to the sound of your voice as well as your facial expressions. Babies begin this language learning by watching and listening to you talk to them, lip reading, copying and mimicking the sound system of your language. You will have noticed that your baby is startled by unexpected noises,

recognizes your voice by turning his head toward the direction of your voice, imitates the movement of your mouth and tongue, and is forming a beginning smile. By three to four months your baby is starting to crack the sound code and will coo and take turns in conversations with you in a social exchange of ahs and oohs and gurgles. Your baby will love being talked to in "parent-ese" more than regular speech and you can get his attention by varying the pitch, rhythm and tone of your voice. Between four and eight months your baby will be babbling strings of consonants and vowel syllables, and you may hear your baby lying in bed playing with sounds and squealing with delight as he produces ees, aas, bas and perhaps even mamama or dadada. Your baby will recognize his own name and be able to distinguish between happy, sad, or angry tones of your voice and will like to hear familiar songs, greetings or books repeated.

Research has shown that parents in all cultures talk to babies in a distinctive way that is designed to help babies learn sounds. Parents' words, sounds and sentences are *playful, animated, repetitive, pronounced, shorter and provided in a babyish voice with lots of positive affect.* This early parent communication with babies is important because it helps babies organize the world and learn to communicate. When parents point to objects and name them, babies are absorbing the language for those objects. When parents name their babies' actions they are showing their babies how their actions influence the world. In this chapter we are going to learn about ways to talk to babies in order to enhance their language development. We are going to talk about the tango dance of baby-directed communication that occurs between parents and babies and how babies "mirror" parents and parents "mirror" babies.

Parent communication with babies is important because it helps babies organize the world and learn to communicate.

Bathing Your Baby in Language

Parents and babies take turns communicating with each other by mimicking or mirroring each other and making sounds back and forth. Parents' playful word game interactions are the best toy any baby could have! Moreover, this kind of play is critical to the social and emotional development of a baby's brain, in particular, for the promotion of language development. Research shows that the amount of language a baby hears during the first year is directly related to his later vocabulary, language ability, and academic achievement. The more you talk to your baby, the better!

The more you talk to your baby, the better!

Be playful

Describing Objects and Naming Actions—Speaking "Parent-ese"

Speaking "parentese"

"Parent-ese" is a universal parent language that babies love (see tips at end of this chapter). It is a language that is melodious, high pitched, spoken slowly with pauses, elongated, clearly articulated, sing-song-like and uses repetition and exaggerated facial expressions. Babies love this kind of sing-song language and actually prefer it over normal adult talk. Don't be embarrassed by the way you sound because it enhances your baby's brain development in the language areas. Why? Because it is easier for your baby to understand your words when they are slowed down, distinct, and exaggerated. Try thinking of yourself as a "sports announcer" giving a play-by-play description of your baby's experience. In other words, describe everything your baby is seeing (colors, objects, shapes, letters, smells, positions, body parts) and doing (actions and the connection between actions and how something is working). Talk to your baby about his daily routine such as when you are diaper changing, feeding or sleeping. To learn to do this descriptive commenting you might try to imagine your baby cannot see and narrate everything in his environment so he knows exactly what is happening. Describe your own actions as well as your baby's actions.

For example, "Mommy is pulling off this sock. Malcolm, there's your toe! One, two, three, four, five little toes. You've got your toe now. Whoops—your toe is in your mouth!" Or, as you play the game of moving your baby up in the air and down again, you can use the position words "Up you go. Down, down, down. Up again and down again!" This helps your baby learn the spatial meaning of up and down, and gives him a visual perspective from up high or down low. You can also vary your tone of voice by using a high-pitched friendly voice when your hold your baby up high or a low-pitched voice when your baby is down low. This will help to keep your baby interested.

Be sure to use your baby's name when you are describing his actions, so he comes to know this is his special name.

This descriptive parent-ese language is critical fertilizer for your baby's brain development and in particular, language and social learning. While you can't spend all of your waking hours interacting with your baby, you can put him in central places in your home where you can talk to him while you are doing household chores and where he can see what is going on while you describe things to him. Try to look for opportunities throughout the day to talk to your baby. Research has shown that what determines academically successful children is the amount of language, or talk, and the variety of words they hear per hour from their parents in the first few years of life.

Saying baby's name

BABY ALERT:
The number of words that babies hear each day and frequency of social interactions is an important predictor of children's later school success and social skills. Variety of words spoken is nearly as important as number of words spoken.

Dual Languages

Prior to six months, babies universally are able to distinguish the sound distinctions of all languages.

If you and your partner speak different languages or if you are bilingual, you can each speak to your baby in your native language. Your native language will likely be the easiest and most comfortable for you to deliver in a parent-ese fashion. Did you know that prior to 6 months, babies universally are able to distinguish the sound distinctions of all languages in the world? However, from 6-12 months babies become more culture bound in their language and will likely only be able to discriminate the sounds of languages that they are exposed to in their families. So early exposure to multiple languages will make it easier for your baby to grow up knowing two languages. There is even some suggestion that the early experience of hearing two languages leads to more cognitive flexibility because of the baby's brain experience of having to learn to switch back and forth between two languages.

Use Love Language

From the first day you were undoubtedly gazing down at your baby and using love language such as, "You are beautiful, I love you." You might have wondered, "Does this mean anything to my baby?" While babies in the first few months can't understand the complex meaning of the word "love," they are acutely sensitive to emotions by reading your nonverbal facial cues, the tone of your coos and voice, and your touch or tickles and learning about the world of feelings. In fact they are absorbing your nonverbal emotional signals even more than your actual words at first. Loving and gentle interactions convey a feeling of caring, love and safety and your baby will likely respond with similar feelings by giving you a smile back. On the other hand, if you are tense, tired, and cranky, your baby will probably sense your tension, and feel the rigidity in your body. They are learning about feelings and behavior. By six months they will begin to understand the meaning of the words themselves which express love and other feelings. When you are with your baby, talk to him about your feelings of happiness, enjoyment, love, and joy being with him. This will increase his understanding of language and is the beginning stage of empathy brain development because he is learning that other people have feelings. This will also increase your bonding with each other.

By six months, a typical baby can experience surprise, anger, fear, sadness, dislike, and happiness. Naming your baby's feelings also builds his own feeling language development. When you notice him giggling, name his happiness. When you notice him watching patiently, name his calmness or curiousness. When you notice him straining to have a bowel movement, name his frustration. When he is crying, name his feeling of hunger or discomfort with his diaper. This will be the beginning of helping to build your baby's understanding of empathy and emotional literacy because you are showing him you understand his feelings and modeling how to do this.

Positive tone of voice

Babies are absorbing your nonverbal emotional signals even more than your actual words at first.

Read to Your Baby

New evidence tells us that babies benefit in many ways from being read to by their parents. In fact daily reading is thought to strengthen the brain neuron connections that form the foundation for children's language and literacy development. In the first months you may notice how intently your baby listens to you when you are reading. He is learning about listening, which is a critical skill in the formation of language. Reading aloud allows your child to recognize your voice, your language pattern, and hear an increased number of vocabulary words. In fact studies have shown that the number of words a baby hears each day is the single most important predictor of future intelligence, school success and social skills. Reading aloud also helps babies develop their attention spans. In fact, in the early months babies are capable of intense concentration that you won't see in later months or toddlerhood. This is because infants are immobile and are mentally searching and scanning everything they hear and see in order get information and meaning. *This is a critical period* of time to nurture this ability to pay attention through reading with your baby. There will also be bonding and calming benefits for you as well as your baby.

In the first six months, read nursery rhymes and books with songs to your baby – and show your baby soft touch-and-feel books with bold colors or black and white pictures. Use the same "parent-ese" language discussed earlier as you describe the colors and objects of pictures in the books. You don't need to read the actual words in the book, just point to and talk about the pictures and allow your baby to touch the book and even to put it in his mouth. At first it will feel like a one-way

Singing love songs and rhymes

monologue, but before long your baby will lock his eyes in rapt attention on your eyes, your mouth, and the book. Your read aloud dance is underway.

Some Tips for Reading with Your Baby

- Read in a quiet place, turn off any competing noises such as TV, stereo or radio; and this will also prevent overstimulation or stress.
- Be sure your baby's head is supported and you and your baby are comfortable by using a rocker or pillow or using your baby's favorite position such as in a sling so your hands are free.
- Use your parent-ese melodious voice when reading –vary the pace, phrasing, voice rhythms and pitch of words.
- Read in your native language.
- Provide love, attention, cuddling and intimacy while reading; look in your baby's eyes.
- Start reading at any page and don't worry about reading all the words in the book; you can make up your own stories.
- If you have other children, read what they like while you are holding your baby.
- Remember, conversing with babies in the first 3 months occurs when they respond to your reading by moving their hands or feet or giving you a body signal of pleasure. After reading a little, allow your baby time to respond and then read some more.

I read to my baby

- By about 4 months you may begin expanding on the book by asking questions or including dramatizations including sound effects.
- There will be variability in individual baby's interest in books, so don't worry if your child does not seem intently interested. Respond to your baby's cues. If he seems fussy or uninterested in the book, try changing your tone or reading a different book. If these new strategies do not engage him, then stop trying to read, and do another activity with your baby.

BABY ALERT

Pacifiers (or dummies) prevent babies from babbling – which is an important step of language learning, so only use them as a last resort after you have tried other self-soothing strategies. Remember singing can often calm your baby.

Talk to Your Baby During Meals, Diaper Changing, and Other Routine Activities

Place your baby in his car seat near by you when you are having meals. During the meal, pause to talk to your baby by naming your spoon, or the food you are eating. For example, "This is toast and it has sweet jam on it. It is good," Or, "This is a spoon I am using to eat my dessert." Or, "Daddy is cutting the turkey, and it smells really delicious." You can also talk while you change your baby's diaper. You can say, " I'm taking your booties off and these are your toes. Here is your tummy. Now I'm taking off your smelly diaper and cleaning your bottom with this cold cloth." In essence you are talking to your baby as if he understands you. Even though your baby does not completely understand what you are saying, there is much about your intonation and sounds and facial expressions that your baby is learning about language.

Describing actions and naming objects

Model or Mirror Your Baby's Sounds and Actions:
Be Baby-Directed

When your baby makes cooing sounds, respond by imitating them.

Being baby-directed means that you respond to your baby's beginning attempts to speak to you. When your baby makes cooing sounds, respond by imitating them. Then wait for your baby to repeat the sound and then imitate it again. This back and forth reciprocal cooing and waiting and cooing again is important for helping your baby learn about language and social interactions. When you imitate your baby's sounds, you are helping your baby understand that his sounds will result in a response from you. In other words, your baby's behavior (sounds) can determine your response. Thus your baby is beginning to learn he can influence his environment with his sounds. He will start to understand that he can do something that causes you to respond to him, and he will delight in this new found power.

Mirroring baby's sounds

Singing to Your Baby Strengthens Attachment

Providing music for your baby also has a powerful influence on babies' developing brains and seems to stimulate creativity. Don't rely only on recorded music, sing to your baby often or alongside the CD. This will increase your baby's sense of pleasure and the repetitive nature of the songs will provide a predictable routine that makes him feel safe. You might try singing a calming lullaby to your baby when he is crying or irritable. Keep repeating the same lullaby or rhyme and you may be surprised to find that your baby calms down and stops crying. You may feel calmer too! You will find some lyrics to traditional songs and rhymes in books or on a web site, but don't worry about having the right words, you can get the same effect by just making up songs and words.

Singing and sharing your feelings with your baby as he responds is part of the baby's brain development that promotes parent-child bonding and attachment. Sing love songs to your baby. Attachment is something that develops over time as the baby feels and experiences the love of his parents and his value to them.

BABY ALERT
Language that babies hear on TV and DVDs is not a substitute for direct social interaction. Research shows that social communication is a key ingredient in helping babies learn and promoting brain language development. In fact, most experts recommend that children under the age of one watch little or no TV. At this age, even educational videos have no real benefit to language development, and when used in excess, may actually hinder development.

Sharing Family Songs

Encourage other family members to talk and sing to your baby.

You can encourage other family members to talk and sing to your baby as well. For example if you have other children or grandparents, you can all sing to your baby together. Perhaps you can sing your older child's favorite song, or a song you remember you loved as a child. Talk with your partner or other family members about family songs from your culture that have been passed down from one generation to the next. These songs can be sung in the language of their culture and they not only help your baby's discernment of different language syllables and tones but also encourage other family members' sense of importance and attachment to the new baby. This is how traditions and pleasurable memories get passed down in families.

Sing favorite songs

To Sum Up . . .

Bathe your baby in language and social interactions with you throughout the day by singing, naming objects, colors and actions your baby can see or seems interested in, speaking parent-ese, describing your own feelings and your baby's feelings in interactions and by reading to your baby. Teach other family members and friends to do the same by sharing with them your baby's favorite songs, stories or rhymes, or what words you think your baby understands. Use your baby's name often. By surrounding your baby in responsive, baby-directed language you will be strengthening the neuro-physiological wiring of his brain language and social development. Remember your baby's brain is incredibly plastic and flexible and this period of time is a critical period for laying down the brain architecture with strong language connections.

Musical games and activities

Parents' Viewpoint
ENCOURAGING MY BABY'S LANGUAGE DEVELOPMENT

I sing and read to my baby

- Bathe my baby in language and social interactions throughout the day—talk "parent-ese."
- Listen to my baby and imitate, or mirror, my baby's sounds.
- Sing to my baby.
- Notice what my baby is interested in doing and describe my baby's actions—be baby-directed.
- Name the objects and colors of toys my baby plays with.
- Put my baby in a central place in the household where he can see the family action and I can talk to him.
- Describe what I am doing to my baby—describe my own actions and routines as well as my baby's actions.
- Describe what I see, hear, and smell around the house or outside—use simple words.
- Make everyday things such as diapering, feeding, and bath time fun rituals and provide lots of talking.
- Tell my baby I love him and share my feelings of joy.
- Smile at my baby, and watch my baby smile back.
- Notice when my baby is distressed, unhappy, sad, happy, or curious and name the word that reflects his feelings.

- Read to my baby—my baby won't grasp the plot but reading helps babies develop speech and thought.
- Take time to cuddle. Balance stimulation with quiet time—gentle kisses can help my baby feel safe and loved.
- Love and show joy to my baby.
- Provide predictable responses.

Points to Remember about
SPEAKING "PARENT-ESE"

- face-to-face contact (12 inches from baby's face)
- high pitched, sing-song voice
- slow cadence
- short phrases
- clear articulation
- repetitive
- exaggerate facial expression (big smiles)
- lengthen vowels (ooooh—sooooo)
- longer pauses between verbalizations (wait for baby's response)
- praise and positive feedback (that's right!)
- use an animated voice tone

SOCIAL AND EMOTIONAL DEVELOPMENTAL MILESTONES
1–6 MONTHS

Remember your baby will develop at his own unique pace. Consider these general developmental milestones.

- Stares at faces (1 month)
- Follows objects with eyes (1–2 months)
- Vocalizes oohs, aahs, gurgles (1–2 months)
- Smiles and laughs (1-2 months)
- Notices hands (2 months)
- Recognizes parents' face (3 months)
- Squeals, gurgles, coos (3–4 months)
- Visually tracks objects (3 months)
- Recognizes parent's voice (3–4 months)
- Baby recognizes own name (5–6 months)
- Coos when you talk to him (4 months)
- Initiates baba (5 months)
- Ready for solid foods (6 months)
- Plays with hands and feet (5 months)
- Baby can recognize happy, sad or angry tones of parent's voice (6 months)
- Baby likes familiar language, songs, rhymes, greetings, games repeated (all months)
- Can recognize a few words besides his name ("all done") (6 months)

Smiling and laughing

- Imitates sounds (6 months)
- Babbling begins (5–6 months)
- Mouths objects (6 months)
- Separation anxiety may begin (5–6 months)

PHYSICAL DEVELOPMENTAL MILESTONES
1–6 MONTHS

- Lifts head (1 month)
- Stares at faces (1 month)
- Follows objects with eyes (1–2 months)
- Can see black and white objects (1–2 months)
- Holds head up (2–3 months)
- Visually tracks objects (3 months)
- Holds head steady (3 months)
- Baby can roll over tummy to back (4–5 months)
- Can grasp a toy (4–5 months)
- Can bear weight on feet with support from adults (4–5 months)
- Ready for solid foods (6 months)
- Distinguishes bold colors (5 months)
- Rolls in both directions (5–6 months)
- Baby begins to sit briefly without support (5–6 months)
- Can recognize a few words besides his name (e.g., all done) (6 months)
- Eye hand coordination improves
- Baby pulls objects closer and starts bringing hands together and transferring objects
- Mouths objects (6 months)
- Vision fully developed by 6 months
- Passes objects hand to hand (6–7 months)

Eye hand coordination

MY BABY'S LANGUAGE JOURNAL

Write your baby's favorite songs, rhymes and stories here as well as your baby's first sounds and imitations.

First Three Months
BABY'S OUTINGS JOURNAL

Write about your baby's first outings and visitors here.

First Three Months
BABY'S HAND AND FOOT PRINTS
Stamp your baby's hand
or foot here during the first three months.

First Three Months
BABY'S PICTURES

CHAPTER 3

Providing Physical, Tactile and Visual Stimulation for Your Baby–

THREE TO SIX MONTHS

Introduction

In addition to providing language stimulation to promote your baby's brain development, it is also important to provide physical and tactile stimulation. Did you know that babies who are touched, massaged, exercised, and held or swaddled often are less irritable, cry less and gain weight more quickly? Physical exercise helps promote your baby's brain development. Moreover, skin-to-skin physical touch also helps your baby attach to you and provides your baby with a feeling of comfort and security.

First let's look at how much your baby is learning about her physical development. Remember in the first month or two, your baby had mostly reflexive movements such as sucking or grasping. Your baby's arm and leg movements were coordinated

Body to body

in response to the speed and rhythm of what she heard in your speech. She began to turn away when she was ready to stop. By two to four months, you have probably noticed that your baby is trying to reach out to objects that she sees but lacks the coordination to grasp them. Your baby can lift her chin and chest if placed on her stomach and she is beginning to play with her hands and suck on her fingers. By four to eight months she will be able to grasp things she reaches for and now can sit with support or on her own. She might even be able to roll across the floor to pick up an object. She will pick up things with her thumb and forefinger and put them in her mouth. Beware—crawling, climbing, and pulling to stand loom around the corner from eight to twelve months.

In this chapter we will discuss ways to provide your baby with physical exercises, massages, baby aerobics and visual stimulation which will support not only your baby's physical development but also her social and emotional brain development.

Massaging Your Baby

It is thought that massage strengthens attachment between the baby and her parent. Not only that, but massage may help babies' digestive and circulatory systems develop. It is easy to combine a baby massage with bath time when your baby is warm, relaxed and already undressed. You can give your baby a full body massage with a small amount of massage oil right after her bath. However, be sure to use massage oil that is unscented, natural, and edible, like almond, grape seed, or olive oil. Avoid products that leave a greasy film and block pores, and avoid peanut oil in case your baby is allergic. If you don't have time for a full-fledged massage you can just spend a few minutes massaging your baby's feet or arms anytime during the day.

Cuddling

Spend a few minutes massaging your baby's feet or arms anytime during the day.

Bathing Your Baby

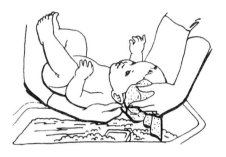

You can use anything you want for a bath tub when babies are young—even a large roasting pan! Be sure the level of water in the tub does not cover your baby's ears while she is lying facing you. It is also helpful to have an extra wash cloth to cover your baby's body because this can help babies feel protected and safe. Don't rush your bath and be sure to check carefully the temperature of the water ahead of time and monitor the warmth of your baby's skin so she doesn't get too cold. During this baby bath time use your parent-ese talk describing your baby's body parts and emotions as well as sing songs and rhymes to make this an enjoyable time.

BABY ALERT
Never leave a baby unsupervised during bath time, even for a minute. Get everything ready ahead of time; don't answer the phone or run to answer the door when your baby is in the bath.

Baby Aerobics

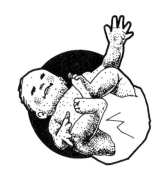

Stretching your newborn's limbs can help your baby to uncurl from the fetal position and to become aware of the existence of her limbs. Try gently stretching your baby's arms above her head one at a time. Most babies get a lot of joy from kicking their legs or pushing on their feet against your hands as they feel the sensations of their body movements. Of course, combining exercise with a fun game such as peek-a-boo makes it all the more joyful for your baby. Looking your baby in the eyes, smiling and being playful makes your baby feel loved, and when your baby finally learns to smile back you will feel loved too.

Baby aerobics

Tummy Time, Head Lifts and Pull Ups

Remember to continue talking parent-ese to your baby during these exercises.

Tummy time gives babies a neck and upper body work out as they try to keep their head up to look at you or a toy or push their upper bodies upward with their arms. Try putting your baby on her tummy with a soft book in front of her to look at. Or, place a desirable object just out of your baby's reach to encourage her to try to reach for it and test out her pre-crawling skills. Be sure your baby is developmentally ready to do this or else your baby may become too frustrated. Crawling is extremely variable and babies crawl in a variety of ways—some even skip crawling altogether.

Baby sit-ups or pull ups also help your baby to gain stronger neck control. You do this by pulling your baby up gently by her arms which forces her to use the muscles that control her head. This experience also helps your baby to feel trust and safety with you because you are securely supporting her. Remember to continue talking parent-ese to your baby during these exercises.

Walking time and Cycling Lessons

Body awareness

Babies are thrilled to experience the joy of walking. You can do this by holding your baby securely under her arms with her face away from you and then slowly help her walk. You can also do this with her on your lap facing you. She will love discovering the sensation of feeling in her legs and you will likely feel her pushing her legs against your legs. Then you can share your own feelings of joy with your baby's discovery of her legs and experience of walking. You can also help your baby develop her leg muscles by putting her on her back and moving her legs in a circular motion like a bicycle. This kind of exercise helps your baby become aware of her tiny body.

She will love discovering the sensation of feeling in her legs.

Sitting Time to Explore

Let other care providers know the exercises and games your baby enjoys.

At six months, babies physically and systematically explore a new object with every sense they have at their command. This includes their mouths and taste, of course! Try propping up and supporting your baby in a sitting position and with some rattles or small toys to explore in front of her.

Let other family members and day care providers or sitters know the exercises and games your baby enjoys. You can even ask them to contribute some notes in your baby's stimulation journal about her favorite activities. This helps them develop their feelings of attachment and importance in their relationship with your baby. This will also be fun and reassuring for your baby and will enhance others' enjoyment of their time with your baby.

BABY ALERT

Don't put your baby in front of television or show them language DVDs. This flashy, noisy, fast-paced structure is not the same thing as real social interaction and may actually negatively affect your baby's brain development and attention span. There is no better way to boost your baby's brain architecture and for your baby to learn than to see your facial responses to her interactions with you. Remember human learning is primarily about human interactions.

Providing Visual Stimulation

So far we have discussed the importance of auditory, physical and tactile stimulation. Baby's brain development is also influenced by visual stimulation. In the first 3 months they are observing everything around them, especially you and absorbing all aspects, especially those objects 12 inches from their face. From 3-6 months, they continue this fascination–in particular, experimenting with the causal relations between their newly discovered physical interactions with objects or people. For example, when you put your baby down on her back on the floor, or in a crib, or floor gym with a colorful mobile up above her head, notice how your baby looks at the mobile and explores it. Babies love to explore how their own physical power affects the object by kicking or swatting the mobile. They may actually get bored with the spectacle of passive watching the mobile moving, but they won't get bored with the sensation of their own physical power and how their body actions affect the object. After a while a baby may only glance at the mobile but she will keep

on enjoying her own body's kicking for a long time. This means that babies don't need constant stimulation—sometimes babies enjoy some private time to watch, explore on their own and to entertain themselves. Remember when a baby is staring at her fingers or toes she is exploring and being curious about how they work. However, it is important to assure that babies are not neglected and are given plenty of parental play, cuddling and physical stimulation.

Provide visual stimulation

Face-to-Face and Skin-to-Skin Contact

Even more than fancy or expensive toys or mobiles, face time can be the most valuable toy you have. Right from the first moments of life, babies are preoccupied with gazing at their parents' faces and movements. By doing so they are processing emotional information and learning about how their own actions affect their parents' responses. They are also learning about their own feelings by watching their parents' facial expressions and mimicking them. Blow on your baby's face to see her reaction. Then smile and laugh at her and wait to see what response you get. Stick out your tongue to see if she will stick hers out at you! Allow your baby to reach for and touch your face. Put your face next to your baby's face. This face-to-face contact and reciprocal dance helps your baby feel secure and safe. Not only that, it can be comforting for you as well.

Stick out your tongue to see if she will stick hers out at you!

Loving actions – tender, affection

Wear Your Baby

Tactile stimulation— rocking, massaging, swaddling

A baby's favorite place is often right against her parent's chest. You can wear your baby on your chest in a sling or front carrier. Here the regular movement of your body and your heart beating seems to help babies feel secure. Did you know that research has suggested that babies who are worn more than three hours a day cry less?

BABY ALERT

Babies under six months of age can be put on a floor gym or mat on the floor while you take a brief break because they cannot crawl yet. However, don't leave them unattended on the floor for even a few minutes if you have other toddlers or animals nearby. Never leave an infant alone on the floor for more than a minute or two. You should always be nearby to monitor. You never know, this may be the day that your baby rolls over, or learns to pull herself forward.

The Optimal Reading Mix

Have you discovered that your baby loves to be read to? While your baby won't understand the stories you read, she will love looking at the pictures as well as listening to your voice. Moreover, we have learned that hearing more words will contribute to her larger vocabulary in the future. Many emotional brain connections are being formed while being read to. This is because reading to babies provides a mix of visual stimulation as well as language stimulation, emotional responses and physical touch. There is some research to suggest that babies and toddlers who are read to on a daily basis will have longer attention spans. When parents read aloud to babies they are repeating words and phrases, describing and talking about the pictures. Babies are actually capable of intense concentration—more than older children—perhaps because they are so focused on observational learning. If you use the "parent-ese" voice methods—this will hold your baby's attention for 15 minutes or more! Reading aloud is one of the easiest and most relaxing things parents can do with their baby. It promotes a feeling of togetherness or bonding as well as enhancing your baby's language development. Remember, though, even as infants, attention span is an individual span--your baby may have a longer or shorter attention span. Don't worry about this, and instead, respond to your baby's cues. If she is tired of reading after 5 minutes, follow her lead and see what else she is interested in. You can come back to the book later when she is fresh. Or, you may find she looks at the book for a minute or so, looks away at something else that distracts her attention, and then back again at the pictures. So pace and adjust your reading mix according to your baby's intermittent attention span.

Reading to babies provides a mix of visual stimulation as well as language stimulation, emotional responses and physical touch.

Baby Games

Tummy tickles, silly songs, blowing bubbles, sticking out your tongue, lifting a baby high in the air and peek-a-boo games are some of the endless ways parents can connect with their babies. This playful stimulation is more than just fun. It is the way babies learn about themselves, others and their relationship with you. Being playful yourself and telling your baby you love her helps her to feel cared for and builds her bond with you. The expressions of endearment and love shown on your face are understood by your baby. As your baby's facial muscles develop, soon you will find your baby copies your facial expressions and your sounds and one day you will get a full blown smile. These fun game routines repeated over and over again help your baby to feel safe, loved, and enhances her feeling of trust and joy in the world around her.

Being playful

Puppet Play

Using small, soft hand puppets (with moving mouths) is an effective way to provide visual as well as language stimulation, different touch sensation, and joyful interactions for your baby. Watch how your baby responds when you use a hand puppet with her. You will automatically use a fun, creative language tone and expression depending on whether your puppet is a pig, or bear, or furry bird. You will soon see laughter and gurgles as your puppet kisses your baby and your baby experiences the delight of your puppet responding to her reactions.

Giving Your Baby a Lift

Babies' perspective on the world tends to be from the crib, bouncy seat, or floor. Lift your baby up in the air so she has a chance to see things that are higher up such as pictures on the walls or leaves on a tree. These will be exciting discoveries for your baby.

Mirror Mirror on the Wall...

Babies are very aware of faces. Letting your baby gaze in the mirror will be fascinating to her, even though she really won't know it is her own face until she is about 12–15 months of age. Repeating your baby's name frequently as you talk to and about her will help your baby to begin to discover she is a separate and unique being.

Rattle Play

Babies love rattles, especially those that are small and light enough to hold and make some noise. Show a rattle to your baby, let her reach for it, touch it and put it in her mouth. Talk parent-ese to your baby while she is doing this and express your delight in her curiosity and discoveries. Be prepared to travel by having ready a bag of toys you can take with you when you are in the car or going to visit someone. Change the type of toys periodically so you are ready for times when your baby needs a new diversion. This will promote your baby's curiosity about her environment.

Be prepared to travel by having ready a bag of toys you can take with you when you are in the car or going to visit someone.

Involving Siblings in Baby Play

Let your child lead the game while you praise her play skills and attention to her new baby brother or sister.

Involving siblings in playing games with their new baby brother or sister is a helpful way to build your baby's connections with the whole family. You can show your older child how you played some of her favorite baby games with her or teach her songs she enjoyed as a baby. Or, you can give your older child a soft hand puppet to use when playing with her. You can start by playing all together and then gradually pull back letting your older child lead the game while you praise her play skills and attention to her new baby brother or sister.

To Sum Up . . .

Providing physical, tactile, auditory and visual stimulation for your baby is as important to strengthening the neuron connections in your baby's brain development as providing breast feeding or formula or changing your baby's diaper. It is essential for brain development and without it babies won't grow, or gain weight or achieve normal physical and emotional developmental milestones. The key is to read your baby's internal state and cues and discover the right amount of environmental stimulation—not so much that your baby is overwhelmed and dysregulated or so little that development ceases.

Parents' Viewpoint
PROVIDING PHYSICAL, VISUAL AND TACTILE STIMULATION TO ENCOURAGE MY BABY'S BRAIN DEVELOPMENT

- Bathe my baby in language throughout the day–speak "parent-ese"
- Provide visual and tactile stimulation such as rattles, mobiles, toys with textures, colors and sounds
- Provide physical exercise such as tummy time, cycling, stretches, massages, pull ups, walking motions
- Give my baby a baby massage
- Provide my baby with consistent comfort when upset
- Play games such as peek-a-boo with my baby often
- Sing to my baby
- Modulate the amount of stimulation my baby receives
- Wear my baby in a sling next to my body so she can see the world up high and can feel the rhythm of my movement and heart beat
- Pick my baby up and hold her high
- Look at books together and talk about the pictures
- Let my baby look in the mirror
- Tell my baby I love her and share feelings of joy
- At four months start to gradually structure my baby's day with regular routines for eating, diaper and bedtimes
- Tell my baby how special she is

I sing to my baby

- Touch my baby in loving ways
- Give my baby opportunities to explore (floor gym)
- Involve other family members in games and physical exercises
- Tell my baby's caregivers what exercises my baby likes to do and what her interests are

Points to Remember about
READING WITH YOUR BABY

I hold and cuddle my baby

- Read at a quiet time when you are relaxed and comfortable–with TV and music turned off (this prevents over stimulation).
- Hold and cuddle your baby when reading.
- Read for a few minutes each day when your baby is alert and has been fed.
- If you have other children, read to them while you are holding or nursing your baby.
- Point to pictures in the book and talk about them, or make up your own story.
- Use "parent-ese" when reading—face to face, sing-songy, higher pitched, slower voice.
- For 2–6 month old babies read books with rhymes and songs, or bold pictures, or black and white picture books. Use cloth books that your baby can touch and taste.
- For 6–9 month old babies read books that stimulate senses such as "touch and feel" books, board books, cloth books, teething books, books about daily routines such as bathing, eating, sleeping, and books that label objects and parts of the body.
- For 9–12 month old babies, read books that encourage children to chime in and repeat words (your baby won't be able to talk yet, but will be interested in the patterns); books that label objects and parts of the body; books that illustrate action words such as walking, running; and books with flaps or

noises. This is a good time to incorporate books into your child's naptime and bedtime routines.

- Remember that children's attention span for books will vary. Some children may pay attention for 10-15 minutes or while others may be bored after a few minutes. Don't be discouraged if your child seems distracted at first. Read for a few minutes and then follow your child's lead to another activity. Come back to reading again and again. Gradually your child's attention span will increase. Several short reading times are just as beneficial as one longer time.

Points to Remember about

KEEPING YOUR BABY SAFE DURING BATHS

- Never leave your baby unsupervised, even for a minute
- Children can drown in a very small amount of water
- Gather all your supplies (soap, washcloth, diaper, towel etc.) ahead of time
- Make sure the bathroom is warm
- Take the phone off the hook and don't answer the door when your baby is being bathed
- Until your baby can sit up unsupported, use a special baby bath
- When your baby can sit up alone, use a rubber non-slip mat if you switch to the regular bath tub
- Use a cushioned spout cover so your baby won't bump his head
- Don't put your baby in the tub when the water from tap is still going
- Be sure the bath water is warm but not too hot; babies generally prefer a much cooler tub than you do
- Fill the tub with only 2–3 inches of water for babies
- Use soap and shampoos sparingly and if you play in the bath use the soap at the end
- Make bath time fun

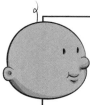

MY BABY'S STIMULATION JOURNAL
3-6 Months

Keep track here of activities your baby enjoys such as looking at a mobile, or having a back rub, or listening to music or being swaddled. Note your baby's responses to you and to other family members or friends when they talk and interact with your baby.

Favorite toys

Favorite place to be massaged or touched

Favorite position to be placed on my body

Favorite exercise (bicycle, walking, arm pull ups or push ups, or tummy time, sitting time)

Reaction to bath time

Favorite song

Favorite game

Favorite visual stimulation

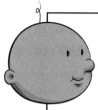

Baby's Viewpoint
THINGS I CAN DO (3–6 months)

Activity	Date	Observations/Comments
I can sit upright briefly		
I do gurgles, oohs and ahs and squeaks		
I smile and laugh		
I found my hands		
I can track objects with my eyes		
I can hold my head steady		

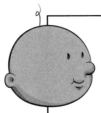

Baby's Viewpoint
THINGS I CAN DO (3–6 months)

Activity	Date	Observations/Comments
I can recognize my parent's voice		
I know my name		
I can say baba		
I am starting to explore solid foods with my mouth		
I found my feet		
I react when you are happy		

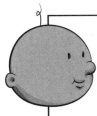

Baby's Viewpoint
THINGS I CAN DO (3–6 months)

Activity	Date	Observations/Comments
I love to be sung to		
I am imitating sounds		
I know when it is not you taking care of me		
I love to explore with my mouth		
I love to be read to		
I have a favorite toy		

3-6 Months
BABY NOTICES AND LAUGHS JOURNAL

Write here what your baby notices, hears and laughs about.

3-6 Months
BABY'S HAND AND FOOTPRINTS

3-6 Months
PUT A LOCK OF YOUR BABY'S HAIR HERE

3-6 Months
BABY'S PICTURES

CHAPTER 4

Parents Learning to Read Babies' Minds–

THREE TO SIX MONTHS

Introduction

In the first six months of a baby's life, parents and their babies are engaged in a reciprocal dance, a kind of tango. This involves parents learning how to provide sensitive auditory, tactile, verbal and visual stimulation and also how to read and adjust their steps to be in tune with their baby's internal states, temperament, and emotions. Parents do this by watching and reading their babies' emotional and social responses to the stimulation in their environment. Babies and their parents are both learning by watching, interacting, and imitating each other. It is a bidirectional dance. Babies depend on their parents to respond to their internal signals or cues–and parents must learn to interpret their baby's cries or reactions to understand whether they are hungry, tired, bored, or over stimulated. This understanding helps parents decide whether their baby needs quiet soothing and caressing, more or less stimulation, a smile or a song, a diaper change, feeding, or sleep. As parents learn the dance steps involved in reading their baby's cues, their predictable responses will increase their baby's experience of security. Parents will also feel an increased sense of bonding and satisfaction with their relationship with their baby and confidence in their own caregiving rhythm. This reciprocal process results in strengthening the emotional and social circuitry or connections in babies' brains so that they learn to trust and feel confident in their environment. This is the beginning of mutual understanding and attachment between parents and their children—a process and dance that will get stronger over many years.

Reciprocal tango dance

I can read my baby's mind

Reading Babies' Minds
Helps Determine the Dance Steps

Since your baby can't speak your language to tell you what he wants or feels, he depends on you to read his mind by observing his actions and mood and listening to the nature of his cries. For example, you might believe your baby has itching gums as his first tooth protrudes because he keeps biting on a particular rattle. So you respond by giving him that rattle when he seems distressed or trying out some ice on his gums. Or, you may notice your baby is drawn to a particular color, or calms down when massaged on his back or feet or when he hears a particular song. You are learning his unique temperament as well as his particular likes and dislikes. You understand that sometimes he needs time to independently explore a toy and is happy with his own exploration and other times he needs some new stimulation or activity with you. For example, you observe that he doesn't seem happy on his tummy so you prop him up and support him to sit to see if he is more content sitting. Or you see if he would

prefer to walk or push his weight on his legs. When you do this, you can also use your descriptive commenting or parent-ese language to describe his actions and what you think he is looking for and feeling. For example you might say, "You look like you are tired of lying on your stomach. It's frustrating when you can't push up very far. Let's sit you up. Now you can see the world. You're looking at the toy bear. That bear's fur feels soft and tickly." This helps your baby's language development and also helps him to know you are trying to read his mind and understand his intentions and interests. The pacing of your interactions and responses is also

When you talk to your baby or change his position or stimulation, wait, observe him and give him time to respond or to explore before making another change.

important. When you talk to your baby or change his position or stimulation, then wait, observe him and give him time to respond or to explore before talking again or making another change. Observing your baby's cues and experimenting with possibilities will help you know what your baby is trying to tell you he needs. Your dance needs to be flexible.

Take Your Dance Cues from Your Baby

 Babies can easily become over stimulated with too much activity or bored if there is not enough. For example, if you have a busy, noisy household with many children and other family members who play with your baby, your baby may sometimes get overly stimulated and fussy. This is why it is important to be a good observer of the cues that your baby gives you about how much stimulation he can handle. This will allow you to moderate or limit the amount of stimulation your baby receives, preferably before he is over-whelmed. On the other hand, perhaps your baby is crying because the household is so busy no one is focused on him. In this case, his fussiness is a signal that he is lonely needs more personal attention or stimulation.

Monitoring babies

Calming Babies–Cuddling and Snuggling

Cuddling

Prior to six months of age, babies need the help of parents to be able to regulate their emotions or calm down. It is not until later in the first year of life that they have some rudimentary ability to self-soothe with a pacifier or their fingers, can physically turn away from too much stimulation, or seek out stimulation by reaching out for people. Full body contact with your baby upright next to your chest and gentle rocking while speaking in a calm voice will help your baby to soothe. Some babies are soothed by being swaddled tightly in a blanket or carried about in a sling. Predictable responses with familiar, rhythmic, physical movements, voices and songs will help your baby feel calm, safe, and will allow him to self-regulate.

Predictable routines

Coping with Crying and Calming Yourself

 It is late afternoon and your 3-month old baby has been crying for 10 minutes. You have checked your baby's diaper to be sure it is dry, fed your baby, and know he is not ill or too hot or cold. You have tried to provide your baby with different toys without success, and your attempts to calm him with cuddling and soothing rocking and singing have not stopped the crying. You begin to feel anxious or angry or frustrated because nothing seems to be working. You are worried about your skills as a parent. All these feelings are normal. In fact, parents are biologically programmed to respond to crying, especially to their own baby's cries. It is no wonder that the crying makes you anxious, worried, and sometimes even angry. This is part of feeling helpless that you have not been able to soothe your baby! Now it's time for you take a break in order to take care of yourself. Otherwise, your baby will sense your worries and your stress which will contribute to his own dysregulation or distress. Here are some steps to follow to calm yourself:

Parents are biologically programmed to respond to crying, especially to their own baby's cries.

- Put on quiet music to distract yourself.
- Put your baby in a safe place and let him cry for a few minutes (keep checking him).
- Take deep breaths.
- Remind yourself nothing is wrong with your baby—crying is his release and this is how he organizes himself and this is normal behavior.
- Tell yourself, "He will stop crying soon, and in a few months, he will not be so fussy."
- Tell yourself, "I can cope with this."

Stay calm, patient and relaxed

- Visualize a place in your mind where you feel calm and free of stress.
- Don't take your frustration out on your baby by shaking him.
- Call someone for help for a break if you can't reduce your stress.
- Build up a support network of other parents and share your experiences with them.
- Find something to laugh about—be proud of your baby's strong lungs.
- Get out the video camera and record a few minutes of crying. Some day you and your child can laugh at how noisy he was.

Remember your baby won't be traumatized if you don't respond to his every cry—especially when you know he has been fed, diapered, cuddled and is safe. Perhaps he is just tired and needs to sleep. In the context of an attentive and strong parent-baby relationship, a certain amount of crying is good for babies. In the first four months the crying may serve to release stress. After four months of age, babies who have the chance to cry and self-soothe are learning to soothe themselves as part of a life-long task of self-regulation. You can begin to see if your baby can settle on his own when he is sleepy. Look for any self-calming efforts your baby makes during these months.

 BABY ALERT

Do something special for yourself.

Taking care of a baby is hard work and tiring and never finished. It is important that you schedule some relaxing and pleasant time for yourself.

Helping Babies Learn to Trust the World

When babies cry, or coo, or flirt, or turn away, they are telling you they are happy or uncomfortable, hungry or tired, or need more or less stimulation. When you respond to his needs in predictable ways and with regular routines, your baby learns to trust his environment—he knows someone will always be there to help keep him safe. If, on the other hand, babies do not have such consistent responses from parents, babies will learn that the world is unpredictable and this can cause them to feel anxious or fearful and reluctant to trust others.

Regularity/ consistency of responses

There are many ways you can provide predictability in your interactions with your baby. First, when your baby cries, you are responsive and determine if there is something you can do to make him feel better. You check his diaper, feed him when hungry, take his blanket off if he is too hot, and offer comfort or stimulation. Second, you regularly play with your baby, look at him and call him by name, and respond to

his smiles and coos with joy and enthusiasm. You imitate his noises and then watch and wait to see what he will do next. You respond to him with delight and continue the back-and-forth rhythm of this tango. Third, you consistently repeat rhymes and songs, often read to your baby, and talk to her about your enjoyment of her. Fourth, you have predictable routines around bath time, feeding time, diaper time, and going out for a walk. For example, when possible, sit in the same place or chair for feeding, have his favorite

When possible, sit in the same place or chair for feeding, have his favorite blanket or toy available, and relax your own body.

Regularity/ consistency of responses

blanket or toy available, and relax your own body. Similarly, try to have familiar routines for your baby's bath and diaper time perhaps with a special song or game. If you have everything arranged and set up nearby, it will be easier for you to be relaxed and focused on your baby during these activities.

Naps and Bedtime Routines

Regular feeding and eating

In the first 4 months of life, many babies will have unpredictable sleeping schedules. This is normal. Their night time sleep will be interrupted by the need for feedings—usually every 2-3 hours. During the day in these first few months many babies will catnap, taking short 20-30 minute naps interspersed with alert periods. While they may be sleeping for 75% of the day, their sleep pattern may be particularly frustrating for new parents because it is erratic and leaves very little time to do anything substantial or get some sustained sleep. Some newborns will nap or sleep longer if they are swaddled and sometimes naps can be extended by "baby wearing" in a sling or front carrier. However, every baby is different and it can be extremely hard to find a pattern to your baby's feeding and sleep schedule in these first months. Hang in there! At 4–6 months your baby's nervous system has matured enough so that he is now capable of a longer period of sleep. This means a stretch of about 5–6 hours at night (though some babies will sleep longer). This is an important milestone for you because it indicates that you can begin to set up predictable rituals that will help your baby eventually to learn to get to sleep. At four months of age you can begin to develop a schedule or routine of more regular feeding and sleeping times. Five feedings a day are average at this age.

Having a predictable routine for putting your baby to bed is important for babies to feel secure in going to sleep and helps them learn to self-regulate. Establishing a routine

Some newborns will nap or sleep longer if they are swaddled and sometimes naps can be extended by "baby wearing" in a sling or front carrier.

around night time sleeping will help babies know what to expect at bedtime. For example, you might have a bedtime routine of feeding, changing a diaper, putting baby in pajamas, reading and singing the same songs before putting your baby in his crib. This routine will help your baby to know that he is getting ready to go to bed for the night. Your day time nap-time routine will be less elaborate, but might involve some of the same routine of a feeding, diaper change, and song.

Predictable routines

BABY ALERT

Be sure not to give your baby a bottle of formula in his crib. As his teeth come in, the sugar in the milk will promote tooth decay.

Providing Security—Sleeping and Crying at Night

At night all babies wake up briefly and cry. In fact babies 4–6 months of age cycle between deep and light sleep every 3–4 hours. As the baby comes into light sleep, he may cry out and thrash about–then settle down again when he finds his thumb. If you pick up your baby to settle him at the first peep, he will learn to expect this and may even begin to wake up more frequently for this comfort. The goal is to balance being supportive and responsive to your baby, with allowing him some chance to self-regulate and go back to sleep. This may mean that you wait a few minutes when your baby wakes during the night to see if his cry is a real cry or just a brief waking. You may also want to develop a bedtime and naptime routine that involves putting your child down in his crib when he is drowsy, but not fully asleep. He may fuss for a few minutes when first put down and then snuggle in and fall asleep. This will help him learn not to rely on your holding or feeding ritual in order to go to sleep, help him realize he can go to sleep on his own, and may allow him to go back to sleep when he wakes up during the night. If your baby is old enough to hold up his head, you might introduce a "lovey" to comfort and help him sleep. This might be small soft light blanket (handkerchief sized) or very small and light stuffed toy. When you nurse or

give your child his bottle, snuggle the lovey in his arm or hand, nestled on his cheek. Then when you place your child in his crib, snuggle the lovey in next to him. At first your child may not notice or respond to the lovey, but soon he may reach and grab for it as part of his sleep ritual.

Parenting philosophies on helping babies to sleep are varied and are often lead to heated debate. The most important thing for parents to remember

If your baby is old enough to hold up his head, you might introduce a "lovey" to comfort and help him sleep.

is that in the context of overall nurturing parenting, your decisions about sleep for your baby will not harm him. If your system is working for you, your partner, and your child, then you can and should stick to it. Whether you choose to let your baby "cry it out," have your child sleep with you, or use a more gradual sleep training method, your baby will be fine, and will eventually learn to sleep. If you are frustrated or exhausted by your child's sleep patterns, around 4-5 months, you can begin to work to change these patterns. *But less than 4 months of age don't expect your baby to have a predictable sleep schedule.*

Remember, right now, crying is the only way your baby has to communicate that she needs something.

Many books have been written which guide parents through the process of infant sleep training. If you decide that you want to help with your child's sleep, one of these popular books listed below can help you establish some new sleep routines and associations for your child. What works for your family will depend on your own parenting philosophy and style. Do remember, that regardless of what you hear or read, *your choices here will not harm your child—you need to trust your own instincts and you may need to test out several theories for yourself before you come to one that works!*

Solve Your Child's Sleep Problems by Richard Ferber (helps to establish routines to get children to sleep in their own beds).

The No Cry Sleep Solution by Elizabeth Pantley (helps to improve children's sleep patterns without crying).

Parents of infants often find that their own exhaustion is one of the hardest things to deal with. Being tired all the time can color your outlook on life and lower your frustration tolerance and can make it hard to be a patient and responsive parent. It is important to find support during this time. It is also important to be tolerant of the choices other parents make during this challenging and sleep-deprived time.

BABY ALERT

Be sure your baby is put down on his back and that there are no bumper pads, blankets, stuffed animals or pillows or small objects in the crib. Once your baby is old enough to turn over from back to front you don't have to worry about turning your baby over on his back but you still need to avoid blankets and pillows.

Baby's Individual Temperament

Just as every baby has a unique genetic structure, every baby's brain structure is wired differently and will adapt to experiences uniquely. This means that every baby has their own particular temperament and complex individuality. Temperament is a behavioral style that refers to the natural or biologically determined way a person reacts or behaves in response to their environment. In the late 1950s, researchers Thomas, Chess, Birch, Hertizig and Korn identified nine traits or characteristics that they felt are present at birth and continue to influence development in important ways throughout life. Some babies will be emotionally irritable, highly reactive to change, and sensitive to their environments. Others will be attentive, easy

and calmly gazing at new toys, and take things in their stride. While environment and parenting interactions can modify these physical traits to some extent, the basic traits of a person are felt to be inborn and stable and do not result from the way a child is parented. The task for parents is to learn about their baby's unique wiring and temperament and to respond in sensitive ways that bring out the best circuitry in that child. At the end of this chapter is a baby temperament questionnaire; rate where you think your baby is on each of the nine traits proposed by Thomas et al. that describe your baby's reactivity to his or her environment. Each trait is a continuum so your baby may be very much like one of the traits, but he or she may also be in the middle or some combination of several.

Easy and Flexible Temperament Baby: If your baby is mostly regular, adaptable, positive, calm and has a moderate activity level you have an easy temperament baby; about 40% of children fall into this category.

The basic traits of a person are felt to be inborn and stable and do not result from the way a child is parented.

Slow to Warm Up and Cautious Baby: If your baby is slow to adapt, initially withdraws and has moderate activity and intensity, your baby will have a slow to warm up temperament; about 15% of children fall into this category.

Challenging Temperament Baby: If your baby has a high activity level, is unpredictable, poor adaptability, and is intense and negative you have a more challenging temperament baby; about 10% of children fall into this category.

About 35% of children are a combination of these patterns.

The task for parents is to learn about their baby's unique wiring and temperament.

Parenting Approaches: A Temperament Focus

I recognize my baby's cues

Since parents can't change their baby's temperamental style, parenting approaches must be accepting and responsive to the unique temperament or cues of each baby. It is important for parents to try to get a reasonable "fit" between their baby's temperament and their parenting style. This can be done by parents observing and learning about their baby's internal state and behavioral style and then altering or adapting their parenting expectations, encouragement and responses to suit their baby's unique needs.

Remember, it is important not to label your baby or child as easy, shy, or difficult. These labels can damage your child's self-esteem and perhaps set up a self-fulfilling prophecy that prevents your child from expanding his or her behavioral repertoire. Perhaps, your baby's temperament may develop differently in subsequent years and this can be influenced by the environmental responses.

On the other hand, knowing what kind of temperament your baby has may make the difference between a happy or a troubled child and between an accepting or a frustrated parent. Understanding your baby's temperament can improve your relationship with your baby because you will learn how to bring out the best in your baby within the limits of his temperament. It is within your power as a parent to help your baby cope with his temperament, to build his self-esteem and eventually come to understand himself better.

For example, parenting the easy or flexible temperament baby will demand somewhat less parental time or attention because the baby will adapt easily to changes in routines, and may not express his or her individual wants. Because of this easy style, parents will need to make special efforts to find out about their baby's frustrations

It is important for parents to try to get a reasonable "fit" between their baby's temperament and their parenting style.

Adaptive and flexible

and hurts and interests and assess what he or she is thinking and feeling and why that is. Otherwise, such a child may become invisible in the family, insecure and not be helped to develop his uniqueness.

On the other hand, the inflexible, hyperactive, inattentive, unpredictable, or easily frustrated baby may seem to have an insatiable need for attention. Babies with these challenging temperaments often leave their parents exhausted because of the amount of monitoring and attention that they require. These babies will need predictable routines, help in preparing for transitions, and outlets for their high level of energy. Parents can work to recognize cues and triggers for their baby's intense emotions and be proactive by prompting a self-calming activity, or changing to a soothing activity such as a story or warm bath. Parents of intense babies will strive to be tolerant, patient, and model appropriate responses. It is important to remove competing distractions when possible, make sure there is not too much stimulation causing them to dysregulate, provide frequent breaks, and try to respond calmly to the baby's intense reactions. Parents of intense babies will need to get support for themselves so they can rest and refuel their energy.

On the other hand, the cautious, slow to warm up baby, will be relatively inactive, reluctant to explore and may withdraw or react negatively to new situations. These babies will also need clear routines as well as encouragement to try new activities and ample warm up time to meet or be held by new people and eventually to enter new situations such as day care or preschool.

Parents will need to make special efforts to find out about their baby's frustrations and hurts and interests.

To Sum Up . . .

Scaffolding baby's development

Effective parents are those who can understand the individual perceptions, developmental abilities and temperament of their babies and read their cues fairly accurately. In other words, parents who can put themselves into the minds of their unique baby and their world viewpoints. The baby has been moving from the world of his mother's womb where he was safe and every need was met and has taken a journey in first few months to a new world of new noises, smells, tastes, sights, touch and a schedule that he doesn't understand. His brain is under construction and he has been completely helpless, unable to even lift his head, or roll over relying entirely on his parents. During this time his parents have helped to scaffold him so he feels loved, safe and secure by providing consistent comfort, predictable routines, stimulation tailored to his mood and temperament, and calm loving. The foundational bricks of his brain architecture and neuron connections have been laid securely. In the next 6 months, he will discover his sense of self—he will be learning how to grab, scoot, crawl and pull himself to standing on the furniture and how he influences others' emotional reactions to him.

HELPING MY BABY FEEL LOVED, SAFE AND SECURE

- Cuddle, rock, kiss, and hug my baby often
- Speak "parent-ese" to my baby
- Try to make sense of my baby's nonverbal cues and cries by checking out diaper, feeding, or cuddling needs
- Try to see my baby's point of view and talk to my baby about it
- Provide consistent comfort when my baby is upset
- Say my baby's name often
- Make everyday things such as diapering, feeding, bath time fun and loving rituals to give a familiar feeling
- Tell my baby I love him and share feelings of joy
- Notice when my baby is distressed, unhappy, sad, or happy and name and reflect his feeling
- Structure my baby's day with predictable routines and responses
- Modulate the amount of stimulation my baby receives
- Touch my baby in loving ways
- Try to be consistent and limit the number of activity changes each day
- Stay calm with my baby when my baby is upset
- Read my baby's mind and respond with adjustments

I say my baby's name often

Points to Remember about

ESTABLISHING A BABY'S HEALTHY, INDEPENDENT SLEEP HABITS

Remember that different parents have different goals and philosophies for their child's sleep. If you are happy with your current routine, you do not need to change it! If you want to encourage your child to sleep on his own, the following tips will help you and your child to meet that goal.

I have a bedtime routine

- Set bedtime and regular nap times to regulate sleep patterns (start at 4–5 months).
- Choose a bedtime that fits your family schedule and stick to it as much as possible.
- Establish a bedtime routine such as: bath, diaper, pajamas, story, song and kiss good night.
- Do the bedtime routine in the same order each night.
- Establish a less elaborate, but consistent naptime routine
- Try to place your baby in his bed when he is drowsy, but not asleep.
- If your child is old enough to lift his head up independently, introduce a small, light lovey.
- Remember babies will not be harmed by crying for a few minutes after being put in the crib.
- If your baby wakes up in the middle of the night, give him a chance to go back to sleep on his own.

- By 4–6 months, most babies do not need to be fed in the middle of the night for nutritional purposes. Many have learned to use nursing or a bottle for comfort at these times. These feedings can be gradually shortened and then stopped.
- Remember babies cycle between deep and light sleep every 3–4 hours. When they are in light sleep they may cry out and thrash about. Before responding to your baby, give him a chance to resettle on his own.

Healthy sleep habits

GOODNESS OF FIT—
MANAGING MY BABY'S TEMPERAMENT

I make my baby feel special

Even if parents have different temperaments than their children, they can still strive for a good fit with their baby and child. A good fit is when parents' demands and expectations are compatible with their child's temperament, abilities and characteristics. The goal is always to manage rather than to squelch or change temperament.

Here are some tips for achieving a good fit and managing your baby's temperament.

- Realize that my baby's temperament style is not my "fault" because temperament is something biological and innate, not something that is learned from parents. My baby is not purposely trying to be difficult or irritating. Don't blame him or myself.
- Respect my baby's temperament without comparing to other siblings or trying to change his or her basic temperament.
- Consider my own basic temperament and behavior and adjust my parenting responses when they clash with my baby's responses to encourage a better fit.
- Remember what I model for my children is what they learn from me.
- Try to consider and anticipate my baby's adaptability, activity level, sensitivity, biological rhythms and ability to sustain attention when planning activities that are most suitable for my baby.

- Try to focus on the issues of the moment. Do not project into the future.
- Review my expectations for my baby, my preferences and my values. Are they realistic and appropriate?
- Anticipate high risk situations and try to avoid or minimize them.
- Enjoy the interactions and the differences in each of my children.
- Avoid labeling my baby as bad or difficult as this may lead to negative self-image and further compound his difficulties.
- Try to distinguish between a tantrum that is temperamentally induced (reaction to disappointment) versus one that is manipulative (designed to get parent to give in).
- Help my baby feel special.
- Find a way to get relief for myself and my baby by scheduling some time apart.

Remember above all temperament qualities can be shaped to work to a child's advantage if they are sensibly managed.

Stay in the moment

MY BABY'S
BEDTIME ROUTINE JOURNAL

Write down your routine for putting your baby to bed at night.

MY BABY'S
FEEDING ROUTINE JOURNAL

Write down your routine for feeding your baby.

MY BABY'S
BATHING ROUTINE JOURNAL

Write down your routine for bathing your baby.

My Baby's Daily Journal
FOUR MONTHS

SLEEP TIMES

FEEDING TIMES

PLAY & ALERT TIMES

FUSSY TIMES

BOWEL MOVEMENTS

My Baby's Daily Journal
FIVE MONTHS

SLEEP TIMES

FEEDING TIMES

PLAY & ALERT TIMES

FUSSY TIMES

BOWEL MOVEMENTS

My Baby' Daily Journal
SIX MONTHS

SLEEP TIMES

FEEDING TIMES

PLAY & ALERT TIMES

FUSSY TIMES

BOWEL MOVEMENTS

My Baby's Temperament

In this temperament questionnaire rate where you think your baby is on each of the nine traits proposed by Thomas et al. that describe your baby's reactivity to his or her environment. Each trait is a continuum so your baby may be very much like one of the traits, but he or she may also be in the middle. Once you have assessed your baby's individual temperament then rate your own temperament and think about your similarities or differences.

My baby's activity level: *This is the amount s/he moves or wiggles or is on the go versus how much s/he relaxes or sits still or prefers quiet activities.*

VERY ACTIVE   QUIET AND RELAXED

1   2   3   4   5

The regularity of my baby's bodily functions: *This is the predictability of his or her sleep times, appetite, and bowel movements.*

MOSTLY REGULAR/PREDICTABLE   MOSTLY IRREGULAR/UNPREDICTABLE

1   2   3   4   5

My baby's adaptability: *This is how s/he adapts to changes in routine, new food, new people, or new places.*

ADAPTS QUICKLY   SLOW TO ADAPT

1   2   3   4   5

My baby's approach: *This is how eager s/he is to try something new versus how fearful or shy s/he is when presented with a new situation or person.*

EAGER INITIAL APPROACH   INITIAL WITHDRAWAL OR RELUCTANCE

1   2   3   4   5

My baby's physical sensitivity: *This is how sensitive s/he is to noise, tastes, textures, bright lights, touch or temperature.*

NOT SENSITIVE   VERY SENSITIVE

1   2   3   4   5

My baby's intensity: *This is how intensely he or she reacts emotionally to things, even minor events.*

HIGH EMOTIONAL INTENSITY   MILD CALM REACTION

1   2   3   4   5

My baby's distractibility: *This is the degree to which s/he is distracted by sounds, sights, or things in the environment versus how much s/he can shut out external stimuli and pay attention.*

VERY DISTRACTIBLE   NOT DISTRACTIBLE

1   2   3   4   5

My baby's mood: *This is the degree to which s/he is happy or positive versus negative.*

POSITIVE MOOD   NEGATIVE MOOD

1   2   3   4   5

My baby's persistence: *This is the degree to which s/he can persist or sustain his or her attention versus how easily s/he gives up in the face of obstacles.*

LONG ATTENTION SPAN   SHORT ATTENTION SPAN

1   2   3   4   5

Parents' Temperament Fit with Baby's Temperament

Parents also have their own temperament and need to understand how their own temperament style meshes with their baby's temperament. Sometimes parent-child temperaments are very similar; other times they are very different. Both similar and different parent-child temperaments may result in clashes or be complementary.

Do the questionnaire you did earlier for your baby now for yourself. See what you find out about your temperament fit with your baby at this stage in her development.

My activity level: *This is the amount I move versus how much I relax. I am:*

VERY ACTIVE   QUIET AND RELAXED

1	2	3	4	5

The regularity of my bodily functions: *This is the predictability of my sleep times, eating, and bowel movements. I am:*

MOSTLY REGULAR/PREDICTABLE   MOSTLY IRREGULAR/UNPREDICTABLE

1	2	3	4	5

My adaptability: *This is how I adapt to changes in routine, new food, new people, or new places. I usually:*

ADAPT QUICKLY   SLOW TO ADAPT

1	2	3	4	5

My approach: *This is how eager I am to try something new versus how fearful or shy I am. Usually I am:*

EAGER INITIAL APPROACH   INITIAL WITHDRAWAL OR RELUCTANCE

1   2   3   4   5

My physical sensitivity: *This is my sensitivity to noise, textures, bright lights, temperature is:*

NOT SENSITIVE   VERY SENSITIVE

1   2   3   4   5

My intensity: *This is the intensity of my reactions or emotions:*

HIGH EMOTIONAL INTENSITY   MILD CALM REACTION

1   2   3   4   5

My distractibility: *This is the degree to which I am distracted and notice everything around me versus how much I can shut out external stimuli. Usually I am:*

VERY DISTRACTIBLE   NOT DISTRACTIBLE

1   2   3   4   5

My mood: *This is the degree to which I am happy or positive versus negative. Usually I have a:*

POSITIVE MOOD   NEGATIVE MOOD

1   2   3   4   5

My persistence: *This is degree to which I can persist or sustain my attention versus how easily I give up. Usually I have a:*

LONG ATTENTION SPAN   SHORT ATTENTION SPAN

1   2   3   4   5

3-6 Months
BABY'S PICTURES

CHAPTER 5

Parents Gaining Support–

FIRST SIX MONTHS

Introduction

Most parents of babies feel tired, and at times overwhelmed and stressed during their first months with their new baby. Because babies have no fixed sleep schedule during the first months, parents are on-call 24 hours a day and not getting any sustained sleep periods. Parents' sleep deprivation plus the intensity of the work involved in continual caring for a young baby can contribute to parent irritability, lack of energy and even sadness at times. Relationships between partners are likely to be conflictual and stressful occasionally. This can surprise parents who may have unrealistically expected their babies to bring continual joy. However, this is a normal response and can be managed by being aware of your mood and expression of it and getting rest and support when you need it. Getting support from others such as grandparents, friends, and day care providers to help you care for your baby while you get the occasional break is important. While you will miss being away from your baby, this break will allow you time to refuel your energy, to rest, and return to your baby with a positive, relaxed attitude. This time away, for even an hour, is good for your baby too. Babies are remarkably sensitive to their emotional environment and to parental stressful responses. They can detect when something is wrong. Research has indicated that if babies regularly experience an angry or hostile social environment there will be negative changes in brain development and in physiological states such as increases in heart rate and blood pressure. Babies also have more difficulty regulating their behavior and emotions in a stressful environment. Therefore it is essential to get support from others, to keep life simple, and to provide your baby with positive, calm, patient and nurturing parenting.

Calm, patient and nurturing

BABY ALERT

When you leave your baby with someone you trust, it is important to help them understand how to continue the predictable routines you have established so that your baby will feel secure and safe when you are gone. Be sure to let them know how to reach you.

Planning for Leaving Your Baby with Others

The first few times that you leave your baby with someone else, it can be painful and difficult to separate. You will likely be thinking about your baby much of the time you are gone. But knowing your baby is in the hands of a person who knows your baby's routines as well as her likes and dislikes will make all the difference. You can start this process of trusting someone else to take care of your baby by sharing with them what your typical day is usually like. Think about what you would usually be doing with your baby during the time you will be gone, and share with your caregiver your typical day notes regarding your usual schedule and activities. You might include information about your baby's eating habits and his sleep and diapering routines. You can also include ideas about your baby's preferences such as what songs, activities, and toys she likes. There is a lot you can share so that you know that your caregiver will be doing many of the same things you do and this will help you feel connected with your baby even when you are away.

If possible, you and the new caregiver will both feel more comfortable with the process if you spend some time together with your baby before you leave. Perhaps schedule an hour together and have your caregiver help you give your baby a bath, play together with your baby, and do a feeding and diapering together. Always try to schedule some transition time when you are going out. Have the caregiver arrive 15 minutes before you need to leave so that you have time to share important information before running out the door.

Protecting

Knowing your baby is in the hands of a person who knows your baby's routines as well as her likes and dislikes will make all the difference.

If possible start by leaving your baby for short periods of time, perhaps by leaving her with your friend for 15-30 minutes while you take a walk, have a bath, go to exercise. Then as you get more comfortable with this, you can gradually increase the amount of time you are away.

Deciding About Work Outside the Home

Individual, personal decisions

Going back to work can be a difficult decision. Some of you may find you are eager to resume a career which you find rewarding and important for your family income. Others may prefer to stay home. Some parents have life circumstances that allow them to make those choices while others may have work demands or economic situations that require them to be back at work more quickly than they would like. These are individual personal decisions and there is no "right" approach, except the one that is right for you. And, it is important to remember that you may feel conflicted even if you've made a decision that you know is right for you and your family.

You may feel conflicted even if you've made a decision that you know is right for you and your family.

Learning About Your Baby's Day

Ask your day care provider to record in your caregiver journal what happens each day.

If you have decided to go back to work, you can feel more emotionally connected to your baby's life while at work if you know and have a mental map of what your baby is doing during the day. Ask your day care provider to record in your caregiver journal what happens each day. These journals might cover routine things like how many bottles your baby had, when she napped, and what she enjoyed doing. Your caregiver can also help to keep track of important developmental milestones that occur. Give your caregiver a copy of the "things I can do" checklist to record when she notices these developmental changes in your baby. Consider keeping these notes in a special notebook that goes back and forth between home and daycare. Eventually, you will have a valuable journal about your baby's time with this caregiver. Give your caregiver a list of your baby's favorite activities, exercises, and songs. This will help you to know your baby is well taken care of when you are away and promote some consistency in your baby's care.

Caring for Your Caregiver

As any parent who has stayed at home with young children knows, child care is hard work! One of the best ways to ensure that your child is being well cared for is to be supportive of your child's caregiver. Make sure to take the time to get to know him or her. Ask how your caregiver is doing, find out what his interests are, give a card on her birthday. Make sure to show your appreciation for the hard work of taking care of your child. As you grow to know and trust your caregiver, you will also feel better about the special relationship that your baby will have with him or her. Also, although it's important for your caregiver to be responsive to your wishes for your baby, also

remember that babies are flexible and it is beneficial for them to be exposed to many different care-giving styles and even languages. As long as your caregiver is loving, responsive, and attentive, some variations in care-giving styles will help your child learn to be more flexible.

Make sure to show your appreciation for the hard work of taking care of your child.

Sharing Your Baby's Day with Partners—Teamwork

Perhaps one parent works full time outside the home while the other is taking care of the baby at home. It is important to find ways for the parent who works outside the home to be involved in important parts of the baby's care and routine. Perhaps the parent who is home with the baby can keep the baby journal of daily activities or developmental milestones that occur during the day. If possible find a time in the evening to talk and share the day's events. Think

Predictable routines

about what pattern or routine you want to establish with your baby when the parent who works outside of the home returns in the evening. If talked about and planned for in advance, this can be very gratifying teamwork. For example, perhaps the parent who has been away from home all day does the evening bath, meal, or bedtime routine. Perhaps this is a chance for the at-home parent to take a break, do something pleasurable or do some exercise. Working together both parents can enjoy the process of parenting and can be mutually supportive to each other. This is important for your

relationship with each other and for each parent's relationship with the baby.

Often the parent who spends more time with the baby feels more confident about caring for her needs. This is natural: this parent has had more practice reading the baby's cues, experimenting with comfort methods, and bonding with her. Because of this, your baby may also be comforted more quickly by the stay-at-home parent. This can leave the other parent feeling left out and ineffective. It is important for each parent to have a chance to develop an independent relationship with

the baby. For the stay-at-home parent this may mean withholding advice and letting your partner and the baby work out their relationship. It may be true that you could comfort your child more quickly, or change a diaper more effectively, but if you always step in and take over, your partner will feel disconnected and may eventually withdraw. This means that your baby will miss out on having the same special relationship with your partner, and you will lose an important co-parent.

Remember, your baby will benefit from experiencing differences in your two parenting styles, as long as each of you is responsive and loving.

Remember, your baby will benefit from experiencing differences in your two parenting styles.

Sharing Your Baby's Day with Other Family Members and Friends

In addition to sharing with partners and day care providers, encourage other family members to be part of your baby's life. Perhaps your relatives live in other cities or countries, but you can still involve them in your baby's life by sending them emails, pictures, phone calls or letters. By letting other family members and friends know about your baby's accomplishments, you are creating a supportive family network who will care about your baby as she grows up.

I am creating a supportive family network

Your Baby's Relationship with Your Caregiver

If you are a working parent and your child is consistently with a caregiver, you may begin to feel like your child has a stronger bond with your caregiver than she does with you. This can be a heart wrenching feeling, especially if your caregiver is getting to experience important milestones in your child's life that you feel you are missing (the first smile, giggle, crawl, word). Know that these feelings are normal and acknowledge them to yourself. Talk about them with a partner or friend. Also, know that the parent-child bond is the most important bond that there is. Even if your child spends much of each day with a caregiver, your child's primary bond will be with her parent or parents. You, as parent, will be the safest, strongest relationship your child will ever have. It is good for your child to establish a close relationship with a caregiver, so celebrate and encourage this relationship, and feel secure in your own relationship with your child.

> Even if your child spends much of each day with a caregiver, your child's primary bond will be with her parent or parents.

BABY ALERT

Never leave your baby alone without knowing who is in charge! If you have a teenage babysitter, be sure you have established some rules about boyfriends visiting, length of time on the phone, and your baby's regular routine, feeding and activity needs. Be sure your sitter has your phone number and has access to you.

Joining Parent Groups

These first parent support groups can lead to life-long relationships and support groups.

Joining other parents in parent groups is also fun and an excellent source of social support. Getting together with other parents who have babies of similar ages can be a satisfying place to share ideas about baby development, learn about new songs, baby toys, and resources, get some ideas about differing baby temperaments and feeding schedules and share joys and worries. Exchange out-grown clothing, car seats, toys, cribs, and even child care! These first parent support groups can lead to life-long relationships and support groups that stay together until the children are adults! For parents whose extended families live far away or for single parents, these groups can be the basis for extended family support.

Social support

To Sum Up . . .

Taking care of your baby is hard work and it is important to keep refueling yourself to have the energy for this work. You can do this refueling by building a support team that involves your extended family, friends, caregivers and babysitter. These people can help give you a break so you get enough sleep and relaxation so you can return to your baby with a relaxed and joyful attitude. Not only that but your baby will enjoy getting to know a new family member or friend and your extended family member will experience the pleasure of developing a special bond with your baby.

Parents' Viewpoint
DEVELOPING MY SUPPORT TEAM

- Take some personal time to refuel my energy
- Do something nice for myself such as exercise, have a massage or walk with a friend; when I recognize and meet some of my own needs, my children benefit too.

I keep life simple

  - Leave my baby with a caregiver I trust
  - Help my caregiver know my baby's schedule, regular routine, and favorite activities
  - After being away from my baby, find out about my baby's activities and routine with her caregiver
  - Support my baby's caregiver with appreciation for his or her thoughtful efforts with my baby

- Encourage my baby's special relationship with my caregiver— remember this is a healthy sign and will not diminish my special bond with my baby
- Encourage my baby's relationships with family relatives and friends by sharing my baby's developmental milestones and special interests via phone, email or texting; even though they may not live nearby they can still be involved in my baby's life
- Keep a log of the fun moments to share with friends.
- Join with other parents to share parenting ideas, experiences and frustrations.
- Keep life simple.

Points to Remember about
BABYSITTER PREPARATIONS

I trust my babysitter

Things to discuss with your babysitter:

- Location of your emergency information (you can fill this out once and post it on the refrigerator).
- Where you will be and when you will be home.
- Your child's schedule for the time you will be gone: discuss feeding, diapering, sleeping, and activities that your toddler likes. It can be helpful to write this down for your babysitter.
- Show the babysitter where everything is and what to do: diaper changing table and where to put soiled diapers, bottles, and how to warm milk, where you child usually sits or plays (bouncy seat, exersaucer).
- If your babysitter will be transporting your child in the car, make sure that the carseat is properly installed and show her how to secure your baby in the seat.
- Review baby-proofing needs and stress particular situations where your child needs monitoring (protection from the family dog, siblings, where your child can and can not be safely placed). This will vary depending on your child's developmental level.
- Particularly if you have a young babysitter, discuss your expectations for his or her behavior: visitors, phone calls, texting, whether he or she can leave the house with your baby.
- Check with your babysitter about her level of experience with children the age of your baby. If you have an inexperienced babysitter, you will need to

think carefully about the different situations he or she will encounter and provide enough guidance to keep your baby safe. For example, if your teenage babysitter has never given a bath to an infant, do not have her bathe your infant while you are gone. Provide clear guidelines about what your baby can and can not have to eat.

- Discuss when your babysitter should call you. This will also vary depending on the experience of your babysitter. For example, you might let an experienced caregiver use his or her own judgment, but might have a teenager call you if your child has been crying for more than 5-10 minutes.
- Let your babysitter know what she can and can't do in your house: are you offering access to food in your kitchen, television or computer use after your baby is asleep.
- Better yet to have your babysitter spend time with you in advance to observe and learn your feeding and changing routines and play interactions.

Once you have covered these things with your babysitter, relax and enjoy your time away!

MY SUPPORT JOURNAL

Make a list here of things you find pleasurable and ways you can provide yourself with enough support and rest to have the energy to take care of your baby.

For example, a short walk, read the newspaper, have tea with a friend, go jogging, talk on the phone, have a bath, go to a movie.

MY SUPPORT JOURNAL

Write here something pleasureable you did in the past week to refuel your energy or feel supported.

MY CAREGIVER'S JOURNAL

Caregiver, record here things she/he has noticed about your baby's daily schedule, likes and dislikes and new developmental landmarks

SCHEDULE

LIKES

DISLIKES

**NEW DEVELOPMENTAL
LANDMARKS**

NEW THINGS TRIED

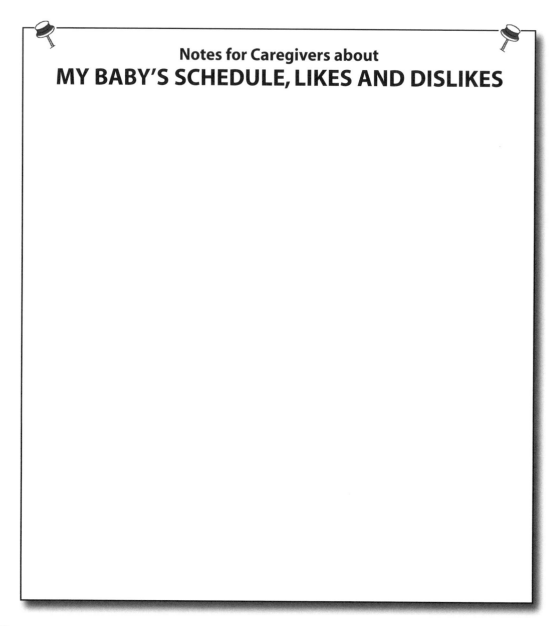

Notes for Caregivers about
MY BABY'S SCHEDULE, LIKES AND DISLIKES

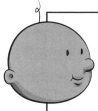

Baby's Viewpoint
THINGS I CAN DO (6–9 months)

Activity	Date	Observations/Comments
I can sit without support now		
I am trying to crawl with my arms but my legs don't work yet		
I can wave bye-bye		
I can say mama and dada		
I can reach for something I want		
I can indicate with gestures what I want		

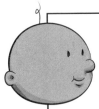

Baby's Viewpoint
THINGS I CAN DO (6–9 months)

Activity	Date	Observations/Comments
I understand "no"		
I can understand what you are telling me		
I can search for things that are hidden or just out of reach		
I am curious and want to examine things		
I can feed myself by picking up stick-shaped pieces of food with my fingers		
I am experimenting with what foods I like and dislike		

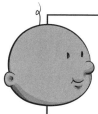

Baby's Viewpoint
THINGS I CAN DO (6–9 months)

Activity	Date	Observations/Comments
I enjoy being read to		
I am drinking from a sippy cup		
I love pat-a-cake and other peek-a-boo games		
I am crawling with my belly off the floor		
I can put things in a container		
I am trying to pull up to stand		
I copy others using a spoon or fork		

EMERGENCY INFORMATION
Post on the Refrigerator

PARENT'S CELL PHONE _____

WHOM TO CALL IF YOU CAN'T REACH ME

Name_____ Name _____

Phone _____ Phone _____

IN CASE OF EMERGENCY

Our 911 address is _____

Our closest major intersection is: _____

OUR CLOSEST NEIGHBOR YOU CAN CONTACT IN AN EMERGENCY

Name _____

Address _____

Phone Number _____

DOCTOR NAME/ADDRESS/PHONE NUMBER _____

_____

[CHILD]'S INSURANCE INFORMATION

Provider _____ Group ID# _____

Insured's Name and ID# _____ Policy ID# _____

EMERGENCY TREATMENT RELEASE

Child's Name _____ Birthdate _____

Any licensed physician, dentist or hospital may give necessary emergency medical service to my child (_____) at the request of the person bearing this consent form.

_____   _____
SIGNATURE OF PARENT OR LEGAL GUARDIAN   DATES OF RELEASE

MY BABY'S CHARACTER

Write here what you think about your baby's personality and character.

MY FEELINGS JOURNAL

Write here your feelings about your first six months with your baby.

6 Months
BABY'S PICTURES

CHAPTER 6

Baby's Emerging Sense of Self –

SIX TO TWELVE MONTHS

Introduction

As you have seen, in the first 6 months babies are learning about trust and intimacy by responding to parents' overtures with obvious pleasure, curiosity, or by showing their displeasure or frustration when overstimulated or when a parent is unresponsive or absent. In the second 6 months of life, babies start to learn about their sense of self in relation to their parents. For example, babies begin to realize they can initiate interactions with you by reaching for your hair or signaling you by raising their arms to be picked up or by smiling at you. At six months they recognize strangers as different from you and start protesting separations from you.

By nine months they are beginning to understand the meaning of words, even the meaning of "no" and developing a beginning memory. They are now expressing

their emotions in even more purposeful ways such as pushing food off the table or screaming when a toy is not available. At this age they are beginning to try out table foods, and you will notice they are exhibiting some independent behaviors such as holding a bottle or cup themselves or rejecting some foods.

As babies start to feel an emerging sense of self and assert this independence, parents need to remember they cannot force children to eat or sleep, as this will likely result in futile power struggles. In this chapter we will talk about ways you can respond to your baby's beginning attempts to assert some control over his environment and interactions with you.

Starting Solid Foods

Around 6 months you may begin to offer your baby foods other than breast or bottle feeding. Here are some signs that your baby is ready for solid foods:

- Baby can hold his head up and sits well in a high chair
- Birth weight has doubled
- Baby shows interest in food
- Baby seems hungry after 40 oz milk in a day or 8 breast feedings
- Baby can hold a spoon

Some Tips to Remember When First Introducing Solids:

- Allow your baby to explore the food tastes, feelings and textures (by smelling, smearing, touching)
- Next your baby learns about chewing movements and swallowing
- Your baby won't swallow new foods on the first (or even second or third) try
- Allow your baby some independence such as holding spoon, or tippy cup, or feeding self
- Make mealtimes fun by playing games (e.g., peek-a-boo)
- Model appropriate eating behaviors yourself (let baby feed you)
- Praise social behaviors and model them (say thank you for sharing)

- Talk parent-ese to your baby during feeding
- Name the foods your baby is eating
- Show a joyful face
- Take turns feeding and talking
- Respond to your baby's cues and don't get into food fights by forcing your baby to eat
- As you introduce new foods, be baby-directed—let your baby feed himself and choose which foods he wants to try to eat
- Combine nonverbal signals to help your baby communicate "more" or "all done"
- Make eating an enjoyable family time; have your baby take part in your own meal times at the family table so he can copy your eating behaviors

BABY ALERT
Breast milk or formula will still be your baby's primary source of nutrition for several more months, so don't worry if your baby does not eat very much. At this stage he is just learning how to chew, what foods feel like, how they taste and how to swallow.

BABY ALERT
Avoid honey (because of risk of botulism), and peanut butter, shellfish, citrus, and egg whites (because of possible allergies) in the first year. Avoid nuts for children under five years.

Avoiding Food Fights—Be baby-directed

Parents are always worried about whether their baby is getting enough food when he pushes away the spoon or refuses to eat. But it is important to take your cues from your baby and not to engage in force-feeding when your baby resists—which every baby does! This will only be counter productive to your goal. Instead, make feeding and mealtimes a time for baby-directed play and communication for your baby—let him smear, touch, smell, and manipulate food and support his excitement and curiosity in this exploration. Remember your baby's first solids involve the baby beginning to learn how to chew, swallow, taste, and feel the sensations of a spoon and food that is very different from breast milk or formula. When feeding solids, your baby will want to hold the spoon—as well as drop the spoon. Let him do this for he is learning about gravity and what happens when he lets go. Is it still there? Where did it go? Feeding time is about much more than food and your baby won't starve. Let your baby explore his likes and dislikes, and know that they will change from one day to the next. It also doesn't hurt to have two spoons—then you and your baby can both have some control!

> Make feeding and mealtimes a time for fun baby-directed play and communication for your baby.

I am baby-directed in my feeding approach

Promoting Self-Feeding and Drinking

Babies will give you clear cues if they are interested or uninterested in eating the food. This is their beginning effort to assert some independence. You can encourage your baby's cooperation by giving him an opportunity to feed himself, and he will often love this because he is exercising his independence. Start with a sippy cup (with water) which your baby can hold himself. Give foods such as lightly cooked vegetables which are soft but not soggy, and other chunky, stick-shaped pieces of food which your baby can easily hold. You can leave the skin on fruity pieces such as apples or pears and you will find toast easier than soft bread for babies to hold. Not only that, toast bread sticks are excellent for dipping.

Let your baby eat at his own pace and get down from his high chair when he shows he no longer wants to eat or is bored with the food game. Let your baby be in control of his eating because this will prevent many future problems over food. Don't worry that your baby will choke if he feeds himself because at 6 months your baby can't get the food he puts in his mouth to the back of his throat to swallow. This is why he spits out! As long as your baby is sitting upright and offered chewable foods with you sitting with him, he will be unlikely to choke. Sometimes your baby will gag but this is not the same as choking and is normal.

BABY ALERT
Until one year of age, infants need either breast milk or formula to meet all their nutritional requirements. Cow's milk does not provide all these nutrients. Breastfed infants who are weaned before 12 months of age should not receive cow's milk but should receive iron-fortified formula. After 1 year, breast milk or formula alone will not provide all the nutrients your child needs; solid foods should be a regular part of his diet and he may be given cow's milk.

Decisions About Weaning Your Baby

The American Academy of Pediatrics (AAP) recommends breast milk for the first year of the baby's life because of its immunological, nutritional, and medical benefits. Breast milk (or formula) is sufficient food in the first 6 months of life; after that solids in combination with breast milk or formula can be offered until the baby is at least 1 year old. In the first few months of solid foods, your child will still get most of his nutrition from breast milk or formula. Remember the introduction of food at this stage is more about the baby learning how to eat and swallow than his nutritional needs.

Deciding when to wean your baby is a personal and individual decision. Some families will decide to wean early, while others may continue to breast feed for months, or even years, beyond a child's first birthday. The decision about when to wean may be influenced by factors such as your personal preferences, work and travel schedule, your health, your child's health, or by the cues your child gives you he is ready to be weaned.

Many mothers make the decision to wean with mixed emotions. On the one hand, it can mean more flexibility and freedom, but on the other hand it also can also represent a loss of intimacy with your baby. Regardless of when you decide to wean your baby or toddler, the best approach is a gradual, gentle process that is flexible and pays attention to what both you and your baby need. When this is done, weaning can be a positive experience for both you and your baby.

Weaning does not have to be an all-or-nothing proposition. Some women choose to wean during the day and breast feed in the evening or morning. Weaning is easier if your baby has taken milk from a bottle (or sippy cup if your child is older than 12

Remember, the introduction of food at this stage is more about the baby learning how to eat and swallow than his nutritional needs.

months) before stopping breast feeding. So it's a good idea to give an occasional bottle of breast milk to your child around 4-6 months (or sooner if you decide to wean earlier). Even if you plan to continue breast feeding, giving the occasional bottle of breast milk can make it possible for others to be involved in your baby's feeding process and give yourself a little freedom from feeding.

Weaning is easier if your child has taken milk from a bottle before stopping breast feeding.

Some Tips on Deciding When to Wean:

- Remember you are the best judge of when to wean.
- Don't set an arbitrary deadline on how long you will nurse; remember every baby weans at a different age and has different developmental readiness for weaning.
- Delay weaning if there are other stressful life changes in your baby or toddler's life such as beginning child care, or a household move, or a divorce, or you have recently gone back to work, or your child has had an illness. Try again in another month.

Some Weaning Tips—Take a Gradual Baby-led Approach

Praising

- Take a gradual approach to weaning; skip one feeding a day for several days to start with (e.g., midday feeding); reduce feedings one at a time over a period of weeks—perhaps eliminating the bedtime feeding last to prolong the special bonding experience.
- Avoid abrupt weaning, if possible, as it can be stressful for your child and cause mood swings, breast engorgement, or infections for you.
- Gradually cut down on the nursing time and nurse after meals instead of before meals (if your baby is over 6 months and is eating solids).
- Don't offer, but don't refuse; nurse when your baby is adamant about it but don't offer at other times.
- Postpone and Distract. Engage your child in a fun play activity during the time you would usually nurse; distract with a snack or walk outside.
- If nursing is strongly associated with a particular time or activity (bedtime, wake up time) have the other parent or another caregiver do this routine with the child for several days. This may help to break the pattern since the child doesn't associate nursing with this parent.
- Avoid sitting with your child in places that are associated with nursing during the weaning process (e.g., nursing chair). Instead, cuddle or play with your child in a new location during the usual nursing time.
- Make sure you offer regular meals and drinks to minimize hunger and thirst.
- If your child begins to pick up a self-soothing habit such as becoming attached to security blanket or special stuff toy, don't discourage it. You can even

Engage your child in a fun play activity during the time you would usually nurse.

encourage this by providing a special object or "lovey" for your child to hold while nursing.

- Be flexible, gentle, and patient. Watch your child's reactions and respect them; if he is having a hard time giving up the morning nursing, you may want to continue for a while rather than force the issue.
- Be prepared to experience a range of emotions, these are completely normal.

Remember there are still countless ways you can provide your child with affection, closeness and security; offer plenty of opportunities for extra cuddling while weaning. Weaning needn't signal an end to intimacy.

Loving actions— tender, affection

Teaching Babies Signals—"More" and "All Done"

I use hand signals

While it is important to be flexible and responsive to babies' cues, it also can be helpful to have some predictable routines that are used to signal your baby that a nap is starting, or a meal is ending, or a parent is saying good bye. We discussed earlier how talking to babies helps them learn how to decode the meaning of language. However babies and toddlers still don't process verbal material very easily yet, so it can help to add some visual cues when you talk to them such as using sign language or hand signals along with your verbal words. For example recognizing the cues from your baby that she wants more or is finished eating and offering a predictable signal for "more" and "all done" will give your baby some control over her wants and needs.

Some child development experts believe that babies can communicate with hand signals before they use spoken words. It is thought that if they can communicate with their hand signals they will feel more confident and less frustrated. Moreover, research has suggested that gestures and speech use similar brain neural circuits and that baby vocabulary improves as their fine-motor finger control improves. So as your baby imitates your hand signals, these fine motor exercises are actually helping their mouth movements and vocabulary production. Therefore it can be helpful to introduce babies to a few predictable hand signals such as for "eat" (putting your fingers to your mouth every time you say eat), "more" (putting the fingers of both hands together and touching finger tips), or "all done" (start with your hands up, and bring them down in front of your chest).

It can be helpful to introduce babies to a few predictable hand signals.

You can start using these signs as early as you want—around 6 months, when you begin solid foods, can be a good time. However, it will likely be several months

Enhancing Communication

Your use of the signs is enhancing your baby's communication skills and is enhancing his understanding of the words you are using.

before your baby uses these signs to communicate to you (and some babies never do). So, be patient, but know that your use of the signs is enhancing your baby's communication skills and is enhancing his understanding of the words you are using. There are many books and websites that give pictures and demonstrations of simple signs. However, you can also invent your own signs—what is important is that your baby has a way to communicate with you. If you and your baby can both recognize a sign, it does not need to be an official sign language sign.

Baby Constipation

Baby constipation is when your baby passes very hard, dry, rock-like stools (poop). It doesn't matter that your baby squirms around and screws up a red face when pooping as this straining is normal and helps get the baby bowels moving. Nor does it matter how often your baby poops—some babies even go 7 days between poops. The important aspect is that the poop is soft (like peanut butter) when it comes out.

Breast fed babies are rarely constipated and bottle-fed babies may become constipated if the formula is prepared incorrectly with too much formula powder to water or adding cereal to the bottle. Other reasons for constipation include giving incorrect solid foods for the age of the baby such as excessive legumes and high fibre cereals, or not enough fluid in hot weather.

Many babies become a bit constipated when starter foods such as rice cereal, bananas and apple sauce are first offered to their diet. In this case, you can give babies over 6 months some fruit such as pureed pears or prunes. Sometimes dehydration can contribute to constipation, especially in very hot climates. In this case, you can add liquid to your baby's diet by offering cooled, boiled water between formula feeds or more frequent breast feeds. A warm bath may help relax the baby's muscles, but be prepared for your baby to poop in the bath!

> A warm bath may help relax the baby's muscles, but be prepared for your baby to poop in the bath!

BABY ALERT
Never give fruit juice (or any solid food) to a baby younger than 6 months of age.

Learning to Crawl—Drive to Explore

Babies are moving from being completely passive and dependent on you, to becoming curious and beginning to try to explore objects in their vision. This can sometimes be frustrating for them because their body control is immature making it difficult to reach the things they want to explore. Getting the front of the body and back of the body coordinated in order to crawl is not easy! You can encourage your baby to use his crawling muscles by supporting his back legs gently as he tries to move. Putting objects on the floor just out of reach will motivate your child to crawl. However, remember that crawling is one of the most unpredictable and varied of the developmental milestones. Many babies have their own idiocentric style of crawling and some babies will skip the crawling phase altogether!

Putting objects on the floor just out of reach will motivate your child to crawl.

Reading Your Baby's Cues &
Brain Developmental Readiness—Be Baby-Led

We have talked about the importance of reading your baby's internal state and cues regarding his interest in eating and encouraging him by letting him have some independence. This same principle is also true for encouraging your baby's physical development such as rolling over, crawling, standing and walking. While you may encourage your baby's crawling by putting his favorite toy just beyond his reach, you don't want to let him get too frustrated trying to reach it if he doesn't yet have the leg muscles to reach it. You may let him struggle a little and then give him support by moving the favorite toy a little closer to him so he can be successful. This is another example of reading your baby's cues and understanding his unique developmental abilities. Remember we talked about the individual wiring of every baby's brain. Indeed, while there are some commonly experienced developmental stages, every baby does not progress in the same way through them. It is important not to push babies to perform tasks their brains or bodies are not developmentally ready to take on.

It is important not to push babies to perform tasks their brains or bodies are not developmentally ready to take on.

Babies at 6–9 months are beginning to discover what their bodies can do. Not only are they beginning to learn to crawl to get what they want but they also are starting to pull to standing position. This learning is all about practice, repetition and your encouraging responses to their efforts.

Baby-Proofing Your House—Complete Safety Checklist

Now that your baby is beginning to move himself across the floor, or pulling to standing, you must be sure you have completed baby-proofing your house. Remember your baby is attracted by small objects and explores them by putting them in his mouth so you want to be sure there are not small objects on the floor or any area where you put your baby down. Get down on all fours to search your house for potential hazards.

Remember at this age, your baby has an insatiable need to explore his environment and almost no impulse control. The best way to keep him safe right now is prevention—make sure that his environment is set up so that he can safely explore most things. You can very gently begin to teach him the word "no," but with no expectation that he can inhibit his responses right now. So, if you have baby-proofed the room and your baby touches the electrical outlet with the plug cover, you can move his hand, firmly, but gently say "no, not safe" and then try to distract him to something that he can touch. Because he will not be able to act on your "no's" for several more months, you want to reserve the word for a few safety-related things (stoves, outlets) and never ever give him the chance to be in a situation where you rely on his self-control—he doesn't have any yet!

Take a look at the baby proofing safety checklist at the end of this chapter and check off what you have done and set a goal for what you still have to do in order to have a baby-proof home.

Learning by Watching and Imitating and Actions

Remember in earlier chapters how we saw that young babies learn by watching and imitating parents' actions, facial expressions, words and responses? This imitation becomes even more pronounced as babies gain more control over their behavior. For example, play pat-a-cake with your baby and watch how he imitates you. This is called "observational learning" or "modeling", that is, the baby learns by copying or imitating or mirroring what you do.

Babies at this age not only learn by imitation and watching you but also by their own explorations and discoveries. It is important to encourage your baby's curiosity and give your baby opportunities to do this exploration.

Babies learn by imitation and watching, but also by their own explorations and discoveries.

Modeling social behaviors & language

Voyage of Discovery Games—Object or Person Permanence

He will be aware that you are not with him when you are gone and will start to miss you and look for you.

By the second half of the first year of life, babies are beginning to develop a sense of what is called object or person permanence. Before babies develop object or person permanence, when you (or objects) are out of your baby's line of vision, you cease to exist for him. Babies who don't have object permanence don't look to see what happens to something when they drop it—out of sight, out of mind. You may have also noticed that very young babies are usually happy to be passed around to many different adults. If they cry, it is usually because they are hungry, tired, or uncomfortable, but they often can be soothed by any adult who can fulfill these needs. Before object permanence, your baby needs you, loves you, and can be most easily soothed by familiar caregivers, but when you are gone, he is not actively seeking you out.

As your baby begins to develop person and object permanence, he will be aware that you are not with him when you are gone and will start to miss you and look for you. This is also true for objects—babies at this stage will look down if they drop something or will look under a napkin if they see you hide a toy. Once babies start to develop person and object permanence, they must learn to trust that people (and

Playing hide & seek/ peekaboo

My baby can trust me

things) come back after they disappear. Just think, if your baby doesn't realize this, then each time you leave the room, he isn't sure where you've gone and whether you'll ever come back. One way to help your baby learn about object or person permanence is to play games like hide-and-find and peek-a-boo. In these games you hide and then you come back! If you do this over and over, this helps your baby to discover that even though you are not in his line of vision, you are still there somewhere. This is not only fun for both of you but also helps to strengthen your baby's emotional sense of predictability and trust in you.

Here are some suggestions of discovery games you can play with your baby:

Baby Games

Play Peek-a-Boo: Put your baby's blanket over your face and say, "Mommy gone" and then wait and come out and say "Peek-a-boo, here I am". Do this again. Or, put the blanket over your baby's face, and say "Baby hiding" and then pull it off his face and say, "Peek-a-boo, there's baby." Soon you will find your baby putting the blanket over his own face and then pulling it off as you repeat the words or pulling the blanket off your face when you hide.

Hide-and-Find: Put your baby's blanket over his toy and say, "All gone" and then take it off and say, "there it is". Or you could use the words, "Good bye" when it goes away, and "Hello" when it comes back.

These games help you form a reciprocal emotional relationship with your baby and strengthen your bonding. You can also help your baby to practice and understand

One way to help your baby learn about object or person permanence is to play games like hide-and-find.

separations and reunions by leaving the room he is in for a few seconds or a few minutes (if someone else is with him) and then coming back. If you narrate your actions, he will begin to understand the concepts faster. For example, "Mommy's going to the kitchen. Right back!" Then leave and come back in a few seconds and say "Mommy's back!" If you consistently do this when you are at home with your baby, then you can use these same words when you are leaving him with a babysitter and he will begin to learn that "back" means you will reappear.

Reciprocal relationships

Making Enjoyment of Baby a Priority—Some Fun Activities

It is important that you make a priority of finding time to enjoy your baby. When your baby sees you enjoying him, then he develops a mental sense of trust in the world and joy in his relationship with you. From 6-9 months your baby has become a charmingly social baby who is laughing and gurgling to provoke your response and attention. He has become more physically mobile and will be testing his fine motor skills by fiddling with toys or food. From 9-12 months, he is beginning to look and act like a toddler, even if not yet walking. Play games that allow your child to practice motor skills, such as crawling, cruising on the floor, or climbing as these will be particularly appealing to him. Get ready—this is the beginning of "I can do it" stage.

Some Tips for Games and Activities:

- Use an empty box or laundry basket for your baby to climb in so you can pull him across the floor as if he is in a car; or, use it to make a doll crib, a house or fort.
- Practice stair climbing under your supervision; although stairs are usually a forbidden zone, they can be used as a way to teach your baby how to climb them up and down safely. In particular, climbing down is harder than climbing up. Help your baby navigate going down stairs feet first and lowering each foot onto the step below. This will be a big thrill!

Being playful

Musical activities and games

- Introduce push and riding toys even though your baby hasn't mastered his legs yet; by learning to propel himself on a riding toy, or push a wagon across the floor your baby is strengthening his muscles and feeling the joy of some independent movement.
- To encourage fine motor skills, get some fifty cent paint brushes and a pan of water and let your baby paint your outside deck. Or, give him some sippy cups or a tea set to practice pouring.
- Stacking things; while your baby won't stack rings in order until 2 years of age, at this age you can encourage him to use eye-hand coordination to put things on a toy pole in any order.
- Make a talking tube out of a paper-towel tube and show him how to blow, sing, and talk through it. Then take turns making noises to each other.
- Use hand puppets to make up stories, sing rhymes, and kiss all different parts of your baby's body. He will squeal with delight as you tell him where the puppet will kiss him next and this will also help him know the words for his body parts as well as help build a rich and stable emotional life.
- Arrange baby visit get-togethers; even though your baby won't actually play with other babies, he will enjoy watching and imitating them.
- Start some art work on your highchair tray; put some whip cream, cream cheese, or jam on the tray and show him how to

smear it all over to make a masterpiece. Name your baby's emotions and share your own with him.

- Let your baby "help" you or imitate your actions while you are working around the house. He will enjoy rolling in the clean laundry as you fold it, mixing a pretend cake with a wooden spoon and empty bowl, or using a sponge to wipe off the floor or high chair tray.

- Prepare a low drawer in your kitchen with baby proof kitchen items. Your baby will enjoy crawling to the drawer, pulling it open and emptying the plastic tupperware, wooden spoons, and sippy cups. You can install a drawer catch to keep the drawer from closing on your baby's fingers.

- Place a plastic table cloth on your kitchen floor or in the back yard and give your baby a pile or tub of oatmeal to play with. Provide a spoon and a few cups and he will enjoy the experience of mixing, stirring, and feeling the texture of the oatmeal.

- An empty plastic swimming pool can be a fun play area (outside or in the living room). Fill it with several plastic balls and place your baby in the middle. He will enjoy pushing the balls and watching the bounce off the edge. If he is crawling, he will enjoy climbing in and out of the pool.

Read picture books

BABY ALERT

You need to supervise and be nearby for all these activities and provide the necessary scaffolding to keep your baby safe.

Making Happy Memories

In your baby happy memories journal write about some of the happy times you have had with your baby. Write about introduction of your first solid food, or favorite game with you. These are fun stories to read to your children when they are older and you share with them the happy memories you have of them as babies. Include pictures along side this memory journal.

To Sum Up...

And so the first year of life has been an incredible journey for parents and babies. Your baby came to you with his own unique temperament and an undeveloped brain which rendered him initially helpless. He could not even lift his head or turn over without your parenting help. Gradually through your feeding, physical touch, visual stimulation, communication and nurturing responses, your baby has gained more brain neuron connections and therefore more control over his body and has begun to notice other things in his environment. He has discovered his hands and feet and found joy in making them move.

The first year of life is an incredible journey for parents and babies.

He has learned he can put many things in his mouth to explore them—and gradually has learned to crawl, pull himself up and walk. Your baby is beginning to discover a sense of himself, ways of communicating with others, a happy emotional life and is developing an intense drive to explore the world around him. Your baby's brain has been under massive construction during this first year—and your responsiveness, consistent nurturing, and positive, synchronous dance interactions have provided the scaffolding needed for a strong neural foundation. You have been determining your baby's environment, which in turn, is sculpting the structure and wiring of your baby's brain and future development.

Points to Remember about
INTRODUCING SOLIDS

6 months

- Introduce solids at 6 months starting with a small amount of food once a day. Until then, breast milk or formula is all your baby needs. Waiting for solids until 6 months has been shown to reduce the risk of your baby getting allergies and, if you are breastfeeding, will also increase your baby's immunity for the rest of the first year.
- Your baby will be ready for introducing solids when he has head control, has stopped using his tongue to push foods out of his mouth, can sit upright and has doubled his birth weight.
- Feed your baby in the high chair whenever you can–not in front of the television or on the run. Be sure to do up the baby chair safety straps.
- Start with iron-fortified rice cereal, which is gluten free and less allergenic than other foods.
- First nurse or bottle feed and then give 1–2 teaspoons of dry cereal mixed with breast milk or formula.
- Don't put solid food in your baby's bottle or he won't learn about eating from a spoon.
- Begin once-a-day feeding at a time when you and your baby are not tired.
- Use a rubber tipped spoon to avoid injuring baby's gums.

Nurturing feeding

- Don't worry if your baby doesn't seem interested in eating off the spoon; better yet to let him smell, taste, touch and explore foods and feed himself with his fingers.
- Let your baby have his own spoon and model feeding yourself with a spoon.
- Don't worry about your baby choking when letting him feed himself. At this age he can't get the food to back of his throat to swallow—which is why he spits out!
- If your baby leans back or turns his head away from food, he has probably had enough or is bored with the food game.
- Remember, babies first need to learn how to chew and swallow and it may be several months before they become skillful enough to be gaining much nutritional value from the solid foods. For a few months, your baby will be getting most of his/her nutrition from breast milk or formula. You can think of offering first solid foods as practice for learning how to eat.

I am baby-directed in my feeding approach

9-12 months

- Gradually increase the consistency, texture, and variety of foods you offer.
- Let your baby choose what foods he wants to try to eat. Allow for choice.
- Be prepared for messes by putting a plastic sheet or clean cloth under his high chair and dress him in a short sleeve top. Remember dropping food and spoons and messing with it, is all part of the learning process.
- Choose foods with no added salt or sugar. Avoid low fat, high fiber foods.

Offer chunky, stick-shaped pieces of food that your baby can hold onto. Soft but not soggy, lightly cooked vegetables are great for baby munching and tasting. Toast is easier to eat than soft bread and great for dipping.

• Stay with your baby whenever he is eating. Preferably, have your family meal at the same time to promote modeling eating behaviors.

• **Most of all be baby-directed with feeding and let your child be in control of his own eating. Make this a time for fun, food exploration, and discovery. This will prevent many future problems over food.**

SOCIAL AND EMOTIONAL DEVELOMENTAL MILESTONES
6–12 MONTHS

We play peek-a-boo

- stranger anxiety starts (7–8 months, begins; peaks at 10-18 months)
- waves good-bye (8 months)
- begins to understand object permanence (7–8 months)
- can say mama or dada indiscriminately (8 months)
- begins to understand the meaning of words (9 months)
- searches for hidden objects (8–9 months)
- will reach out to objects and indicate wants with gesture (8–9 months)
- jabbers (9 months)
- plays patty-cake and peek-a-boo (10–11 months)
- says mama and dada to correct parent (10–11 months)
- understands about 50 words but cannot say them (at 12 months) (action verbs, eating, bath time etc.)
- discovers self in mirror

PHYSICAL DEVELOPMENTAL MILESTONES
6–12 MONTHS

- sits without support (7 months)
- starts trying to crawl (7–8 months)
- stands while holding onto something (8–9 months)
- gestures and points at objects (8–9 months)
- will reach out to objects and indicate wants with gesture (8–9 months)
- pick up small object with thumb and forefinger and bring to mouth (9 months)
- turns pages of book (9 months)
- drinks from sippy cup and eats with fingers (9 months)
- crawls well with belly off floor (10 months), but crawling is extremely variable and babies have a variety of ways of mastering this skill. Some drag one foot, some do a "commando" crawl, and some skip crawling and go straight to cruising. As long as your baby is meeting other developmental milestones, chances are that variations in your child's crawling schedule and style are completely normal.
- puts objects in container (11 months)
- stands alone briefly (11 months)
- cruises (12 months)

Mastering skills

MY BABY'S FEELINGS JOURNAL

Write here some stories about your baby's expressions of emotions.

**FIRST JOYS
AND AFFECTIONS**

FIRST SADNESS

FIRST ANGER

FIRST FEARS

My Happy Memories Journal
6–12 MONTHS

Record some of your happy memories here about your baby's first discoveries and explorations. Record your baby's favorite games, stories, songs and foods. Keep these to read to your child when he or she is older.

My Home Baby-Proofing Checklist

Take a look at this checklist and check off that you have done all these things.

❑ I have checked to see that small objects (coins, safety pins, marbles, grapes, peanuts, popcorn, keys etc.) and plastic bags are not around for my baby to find. Objects that can fit through a toilet paper tube are choking hazards.

❑ I have taken an infant CPR class

❑ All poisonous substances including cleaning products, shampoos etc. are in latched or locked cupboards

❑ Poisonous houseplants have been removed, or are up high

❑ I wash rattles and baby's toys in the dishwasher

❑ Infant seat is a federally approved, installed correctly with rear facing seat in back that I always use when transporting my infant in the car

❑ I am vigilant about watching my baby at all times

❑ I never leave my baby alone in the bath, on the bed, on the changing table, or in the car even for a minute

❑ A baby gate has been placed at the top and bottom of stairs

❑ Guards have been put around fireplaces or heaters and over electrical outlets

❑ My baby's crib does not have small objects in it, blankets, pillows or stuffed toys; crib boards have no more than 2-3/8 inches between them

❑ I put my baby on his back to sleep

- ❑ My baby sleeps in fire retardant sleepwear
- ❑ I have installed a smoke detector
- ❑ I have set my hot water below 120 degrees F
- ❑ I never leave my child alone with a pet
- ❑ I have placed a set of emergency numbers next to my phone

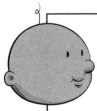

Baby's Viewpoint
THINGS I CAN DO (9–12 months)

Activity	Date	Observations/Comments
I recognize my parent from other adults		
I have discovered myself in the mirror		
I can wave bye-bye		
I can say mama and dada to correct parent		
I can search for something that is hidden		
I can jabber		

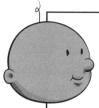

Baby's Viewpoint
THINGS I CAN DO (9–12 months)

Activity	Date	Observations/Comments
I understand "no"		
I can understand what you are telling me		
I can reach out for what I want		
I am curious and want to examine things		
I can pick up a small object with my fingers		
I like "touchy-feely" books		

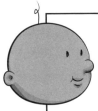

Baby's Viewpoint
THINGS I CAN DO (9–12 months)

Activity	Date	Observations/Comments
I recognize my favorite foods and trying new flavors		
I am drinking from a sippy cup and like to feed myself with a spoon		
I love pat-a-cake and other peek-a-boo games		
I am crawling with my belly off the floor		
I can pick up foods accurately using fingers and hands		
I can stand alone briefly		
I am cruising		

MY CAREGIVER'S JOURNAL

Caregiver records here things she/he has noticed about your baby's daily schedule, likes and dislikes and new developmental landmarks

SCHEDULE

LIKES

DISLIKES

NEW DEVELOPMENTAL LANDMARKS

NEW THINGS TRIED

Notes for Caregivers about
MY BABY'S SCHEDULE, LIKES AND DISLIKES

Age of Baby____Months
BABY'S PICTURES

LETTER TO MY BABY

Write a letter here to your baby about your thoughts and feelings and hopes.

Dear _____,